Turn That
Damned Thing
Off

Previously published book

WE DIE AT DAWN

GENE KLAVAN

Turn That Damned Thing Off

AN IRREVERENT LOOK AT TV'S IMPACT ON THE AMERICAN SCENE

THE BOBBS-MERRILL COMPANY, INC.

INDIANAPOLIS   NEW YORK

The Bobbs-Merrill Company, Inc.
Indianapolis   New York
Copyright © 1972 by Gene Klavan
All rights reserved
Library of Congress Catalogue Card Number 78–173217
Designed by Jack Jaget
Manufactured in the United States of America

To the Five Zany Madcaps

Contents

Turn That
Damned Thing
Off

CHAPTER ONE

Whereas and Whatfor

Things are going to be a lot different from now on. Actually, things have always been a lot different from now on, but we were not there when they were going to be a lot different. Therefore, to sum up, these are different things that are going to be different.

Ordinarily the preface, the foreword and the acknowledgments of a book such as this one would have been located some pages prior to this point. But you would have forged ahead, ignoring those pages as one ignores the printed directions supplied with new electrical appliances. There is entirely too much forging these days. There are also too many appliances and too many instructions.

Therefore, so that the important personal matters and gratuities which must be included are not lost in a preface, a foreword, an introduction, they have been placed here. To be lost here.

Most of what you will find is the truth or what I

predict, envision or diagnose as the truth. Of course some of the truth has been fictionalized. I admit that my intent is to expedite the message so that you will agree with me more quickly than you might have if I had dredged up and detailed the facts for you.

Everything included has been researched. The assertions and conclusions that have not been scrupulously researched or personally attested have been lovingly invented. Bibliographies are so dull, and how many people care to spend time with bibliography freaks anyway?

The important objective is that you ultimately admit to the accuracy of virtually everything contained herein and that you enrich your life by avoiding the contemplation, meditation and consideration of subjects in which you have not the slightest interest.

In America today more people are doing and saying than are doing and writing. There is so much opportunity for philosophizing and editorializing in broadcast words that the impact of the printed word has been relegated to a secondary status. Consequently, people who should be writing are speaking on radio and television programs; and people who should be doing anything but what they are doing are writing their strange theories and remarkable inanities to fill the gap left by the speakers.

I have been fortunate enough to have had a radio-television platform continuously for the past twenty-five years, and I can tell you it is difficult to make an impression when your words are written on air. Quote me one thing that your favorite long-time telecaster or broadcaster has said—besides his opening line or his sign-off. Even people who have heard me the very same morning on WNEW Radio, New York, often say to me, "What did you say?"

I have hammed, reported, recorded, written and ad-libbed on the air, and between dabbling and fiddling, scrambling and finagling I have managed to trespass through most phases of TV and radio broadcasting from start to finish. With this involvement in mass media, through a tenure longer than many celebrated per-former-writers, I have managed to remain unbowed and obscure. There is a limited series of conclusions you can draw from such an achievement: (1) Either we get what we deserve in this life, (2) there is justification to ask, "What did you say?" or (3) so far I haven't said anything.

The problem with talking shop has always been that it eliminates anyone from the conversation who is not employed in the shop. I have always reminded colleagues who work in the mass media that it is incumbent upon us to remember that not everybody lives in a radio-tele-vision world. I have always deplored the proud but re-strictive reference to "*our* business."

Now it has occurred to me that I am wrong. It turns out that everybody does live in a television-radio world. "*Our* business" is everybody's business. It happened so gradually, this subjugation of the nation's life style to electronics, that most people simply assumed it was always that way. Since I had lived in a radio-television world for many years, I decided it was my obligation to illuminate the transformation for you. Perhaps it was not dedication so much as a more simple motivation, the fact that there might be a little money in it.

There are daily pronouncements and weekly observa-tions that are being made by recognized authorities on communications. Most of the observations thrown out should be thrown out because the recognized authorities on communications seem to be interested only in communicating with each other. Instead, I offer you the observations of a working, dedicated, unbiased, con niving, revengeful, embittered, cynical, romantic, not bad-looking broadcaster.

It is customary to thank the myriad of devoted, industrious people who have assisted and nurtured the author in his hours of creation. I believe that most of the people who volunteered information would prefer to remain nameless. Those whom I have quoted without their permission I refuse to acknowledge.

To the tremendous number of listeners who used to ask, "What did you say?" I offer my appreciation for an opportunity to explain. To my loving wife, Phyllis, I leave my sneakers.

To the rest of you who are about to embark on this adventure into the unknown, I invite you to call me when you are in New York, and you can treat me to lunch while we discuss my blatant misconceptions.

G. K.

New York

CHAPTER ONE

Again

The anchorman opens the seven-o'clock news on all channels with the lead item "Radicals dumped tea from a ship in Boston Harbor into the Charles River. The sailors of the Royal Navy were dumped into the drink along with the best of Sir Thomas Lipton and Tender Leaf." Films of the damage are shown, and an interview with the local constabulary seems to indicate that it was those crazies, Sammy Adams, Johnny Hancock—the one with the fancy handwriting who has been scribbling obscenities all over the Customs House—and that wild Revere kid.

But the anchorman informs us that the King has made no statement. HRH has spent the day at the Ascot racetrack reviewing the horses and praising the benefits to be derived from athletics for all the good, clean kids who participate in them.

With fifteen microphones amassed before her face, Mrs. Adams, Sammy's mother, is harassed by the report-

ers into voicing her reaction to the event. Fortunately
she has had a chance to have her wig steamed and her
face pinched at the local beauty salon. She is dressed
in the latest from Liverpool. She is slightly hostile but
seems unafraid. Her lips quiver as she speaks defiantly,
directly into the camera.

"My son Sammy a revolutionary? His father and I, we
gave him everything. We stinted on plenty for ourselves.
He's not a bad boy. But kids today—listen, you send a
kid to Harvard, he learns things, you know what I mean.
. . . I guess . . . I guess he got in with a bad crowd. You
know the young people today. They're not like we were;
they get involved. All I know, we did the best we could."

Continuing coverage of the story, John Hancock, Sr.,
an insurance broker, declares that his son hasn't been
home for three months, that the boy set out for a Rock
festival at Plymouth and hasn't been heard from since.
But the father insists that, although he may not agree
with his son, the elder Hancock will stand behind him
with the strength of Gibraltar.

We cut to the Governor, who, the anchorman tells us,
speaks for the King. It is said that the Governor always
handles the unpleasant tasks for the King. In fact, he
usually expresses the Royalist point of view, which the
King publicly eschews. The Governor stands for his
statement to the networks. "These pusillanimous punks,
these vitriolic vipers of vituperative violent vandalism,
must realize that their desecrational dissension is merely
a lie to the rest of the world. The precipitous precocity
abroad in the land is a myth, a myth the radicals are trying to foment. We should never have let these young
people go to college. Education is bad for most people."

He continues, hoping to pacify the bulk of the people, "Most of the colony, the majority of which is silently pleased by the King, wants only the harmony that the Colonial dream has promised for this, the greatest reign in the history of monarchy."

With the next development another tense day ensues. Not good. It is revealed by the correspondent in Boston that a customs commissioner, wielding a heavy club, has beaten radical youth leader Jim Otis to a bloody pulp. Otis is on the critical list. In a disturbing film clip—which is really quite amazing in its clarity, considering Japanese equipment had not been imported yet—Jim Otis, a fairly reasonable leader of the crazies, is shown being smashed to the ground, while other rebels are forced back by a vicious attack from a heavy cordon of Redcoats.

Immediately from New Hampshire to Georgia a wave of antagonism galvanizes against the repressive measures of the government. In Virginia, Pat Henry and Tom Jefferson, who had been considered moderate in their opposition to the Establishment, are infuriated by the attacks and begin to organize action against the government.

"This is a clear case of overreaction on the part of the authorities. I hold that truth to be self-evident!" Jefferson says in a brief statement to the correspondent from Richmond TV. Pat Henry is more clamorous. "I don't know what the hell the rest of y'all are going to do," he says, "but I say it's the pigs or me!"

Moderates, appalled by the continuous TV accounts of repression, join the radicals. Opinion shifts so rapidly that the Mother Country decides to attempt a forceful pacification. Mother Country sends military advisers to advise the people to cut it out or else.

Guerrilla action everywhere. Mother Country sends more advisers. The more advisers, the more unification against the Mother Country. A hero is found by TV. Every night another clip appears of General George "Old Wooden Teeth" Washington urging more and more action by the partisans against the Mothers.

Most of the people are inclined to look the other way; they really do not want to get involved. Through TV, however, everybody is drawn into the situation. Songs are written and played. "Over Here" and "I Left a Part of My Heart in That Carton in Boston Harbor" are heard incessantly on the air. Beautiful milkmaids are dressed in Colonial blue and sent out to recruit men from the fields and farms and villages—but not until the girls are nationally known as a result of appearances on the late-night "Aaron Burr Show." There is no hiding. Everyone sees what is going on.

If the citizen doesn't watch the news broadcasts, if he doesn't follow the customarily lifeless Sunday discussion shows such as John Adams's "Face the Colonies," then he cannot escape the war on the entertainment programs. The "Craft Comedy Hour," for example, features comedians like Benny Franklin and his funny eyeglasses who brings the battle home with his acerbic topical wit.

There is, as they say on all of the enlistment commercials, no turning back; everybody is in it. The Mother Country begins to realize that the colonies are united and that it would be an enervating, fruitless struggle and slowly disengages her forces, deploying them to other colonies, such as Ireland, where the inhabitants are inclined to be more appreciative. In nine months the embryonic nation is born, free.

Right? Right—unless the Mothers had seized the television facilities, commandeered the news capabilities, inhibited the free flow of instantaneous information and entertainment. Then there would have been a different end to the story. The war might have lasted not nine months but who knows how long as the Mothers attempted to convince the populace that secession was dangerous, that such a course might result in the end of the Empire, one colony after another resorting to secession like a row of standing dominoes.

But that was 1773 and what did they know?

Fortunately, we are not talking politics; we are talking about something masquerading as communications. If we were discussing politics, you could dispute my opinions. But we are going to investigate the changes in the life we lead because of the unconscious predicament in which television has placed us. Therefore, you will simply have to agree with me and accept everything I say as gospel unless you are an atheist. If you are an atheist, you have no one to blame but yourself.

Television is the most important force in the United States. There is no simpler way to say it. You could read Innis and McLuhan and the other pundits who have revealed in esoteric brilliance their marvelously abstruse postulates, but when it comes down to the frightening simplicity of what all that jazz means, it is this: Television is the most important outside force in our lives. Where it is is only the beginning of where it is going. The potential, which we shall guess later on, is both so heady and so frightening that we might be well advised to demand that legislative means be taken by our elected officials to make the whole damned thing illegal.

Television connected the entire country, introduced the people of the cities to the people of the rural areas, showed the different ethnic groups to each other, brought the economic classes face to face. Television brought reality to us right where we live. And then television pulled one of the great switcheroos of all time.

A decade or so ago you could live your own life, but now you are living my life and I am living yours. We share the same reality every day, brought into our homes for all to see without any restrictive ratings to separate the child from the adult. With television, you don't have to be accompanied by a parent to see the raunchiness of reality, all reality, some of it so spectacular that there is no fiction to top it that the mind can conceive.

The incredible spasms of reality we have seen in our own homes, in black and white and color: the living and dying, the crazy people who have danced across our eyes for our viewing and listening pleasure via the magic box! The incomparable immediacy of TV transmission blasted the newspapers from their pedestals. With the reality of people being launched to the pick-up area of our living rooms, prohibitions and restrictions began to dissolve.

Words that were heard only behind the house became words you heard around the house every day. And reality, when it was projected between the virus-cold commercial and the ad for dog food that doesn't look like dog food—reality when it was seen next to "Lassie" or "Movie of the Week"—became just another show.

Startling, revolutionary, yet small enough to fit on a belly telly, it became a show. Presidents and kings, assassinations and retributions, crimes and punishment, laughter and screams, wash and dry, all of it came to us where we lived in our little home theater. The Great Reality Show.

What a switch! Television, which brought reality into the home, turned reality into another show on television. Everything on television is a show. There is little differentiation between reality and the adjacent show, except a station break. Unconsciously, reality became entertainment just as everything that appears on television is an entertainment. If the mind has a tendency to boggle, it may as well boggle on this idea as anything else: If reality is entertainment, then we're all in show business. Everybody—you and I and everybody in the world—is in the entertainment business. Everybody's in the act.

But what happens now, if reality is entertainment, when we get bored with the Great Reality Show on television? How can you provide entertainment now that everybody is entertainment?

When the greatest show on earth is reality, do you have to give away free passes for fantasy? When even the kids know all the punch lines, what do we do for laughs?

Since everybody is in show business, let's find out what is happening to show business. You may protest that there are more urgent, more vitally climactic questions that should be enunciated, even prettier questions that may be posed in a world of crumbling institutions, deteriorating ecological foundations and unfettered bouncing boobs.

But somebody once said—was it you?—that in America everybody has two businesses, his own and show business. Accordingly, you're in this thing as deeply as I am, and we'd better find out what's going on.

CHAPTER TWO

What to Do
Till the
Show Doctor
Comes

Don't be so complacent about the changes wrought in our society by this demon television. Don't sit back and remark how ridiculous is the posturing of people who are rushing to become stars in the tele-reality that has become our way of life. You cannot prevent it. This whole business affects you even if you are plunged into it involuntarily. The cognoscenti are aware that specialists have already carved a niche in the electronic show-business mountain. Doctors of all varieties, from medical to philosophy, are appearing on talk shows, panel shows and public-service discussion shows. Even more frequent are their appearances on closed-circuit television—television meetings or occasions that are transmitted within a building or to a limited audience. Through intense exposure to the cameras they are developing polish, class in their performances.

The business publications have all noted the increasing activity in the closed-circuit biz, remarking that doctors and dentists, scientists, businessmen and engineers are becoming as visible on the closed-circuit circuit as they used to be on the golf courses.

And class tells. The professional person who is prepared for his appearance comes off looking like a professional. You can always tell a professional.

A true story will illustrate the point. I had the occasion to be involved in a TV commercial that was a classic usage of the average person. This particular commercial was for the copying machine that has been an historic winner in the U.S., the name of which it would be unfair to divulge. But it begins with an X.

In order to illustrate the ease, the simplicity with which the machine could be utilized, an actual working copying machine was set up in an actual working shopping center in Westchester County, New York, adjacent to the New York Thruway. It was a well-known shopping center, well established and conducive to large throngs of shoppers.

The concept of the commercial was that the machine was to talk to shoppers strolling by and to invite them to try it out, to see how ridiculously simple the machine was to operate. Obviously since the machine could not talk, a voice had to be piped in to ad-lib with the passersby. I was the source of that voice. Located in a truck, hidden behind a special panel, I could see the shoppers but they were unable to see me or my microphone. The hidden camera, also invisible to the subjects of our film, was next to me in the truck.

We filmed throughout the day, and the results were largely disappointing. Not disappointing in the way that you would think, that people would look at the copier which invited them to try it out and respond, "Bullshit, you're a trick!" What was disappointing was that most people were so shy they were unable to respond at all. Several children were anxious to try the 2400 copier, but their parents shied away. Of course, the machine was forced to say, "Get away, kid, you bother me," because children do not rent or buy copying machines. Most children anyway.

But. There was one strolling shopper who was spectacular. It was worth the entire day for the crew and myself to see the manner in which this person responded. He talked to the machine; he was lucid and enthusiastic when he found how simple was the machine to operate, and his reactions were animated and convincing. We did not know his actual occupation; the briefcase he carried gave us no clue. All we knew was that the man was a pro. His was the only episode worth using.

Unfortunately, late in the afternoon, the police came by and arrested the performing person for "flag waving," the police technical term for a person's exposing himself in public. Since we could not wait for his case to be heard, we were forced to discard his scene. But the story is true and so is the conclusion: You can always tell a pro.

I think the point I am trying to impress on you is that if you are a professional, there are certain reactions which must come from you as if they were natural, even if they are, in reality, considered, practiced and previously used responses.

Television, unlike radio, does not allow you to hide behind your voice and the imagination of the audience. If you are a professional, you know that some manipulation is possible, some conditioning that will allow you to give the impression that you are not giving an impression. I repeat, if you are a professional.

One more incident, which might be valuable, may illustrate our direction. I had written a book that I was attempting to promote via television performances. One of the programs on which I desired to appear to promote the book was a late-night talk show. It is incidental which one; they all sell books. Authors are constantly requesting appearances. The late-night programs feature talks and it is their overwhelming fear that an author may be a hell of a writer but a poor talker. Just holding the book up to the camera while the author bores on is great for the author but inclined to be dull for the audience.

The talent coordinator of the program interviewed me to make sure I was a talker. Since I had been on radio and TV in New York for some fifteen years at the time, I had a slight edge on talking. The coordinator mentioned, however, that before I met the MC, an extremely talented performer and bright interviewer, he would appreciate it if I would compile some stories, some anecdotes that would guarantee interesting talking on the program. In such a way the MC could be briefed by his large research staff and lead me into the stories, effortlessly and naturally. The MC's reaction was, of course, to be ad-lib, because he was a pro.

Then I made a mistake. I told the talent coordinator that the producer of the program might be of some help; he was well acquainted with my work.

Shortly before my scheduled appearance I was informed that said appearance was canceled. I would not be hawking my book on that show. It seems the producer knew my work and hated it. There is a moral here and I believe it can best be expressed in simple terms to tie it into the other story about the flag waver: If you are going to be a pro, don't expose yourself all the way.

But what if you are not a professional?

What, you ask, what has this to do with you? You are the ordinary person, the viewer, the observer, the voyeur, the watcher. The answer is, no longer. And this is the most important point in this whole recitation if there is a point in this whole recitation. There is a good chance that you will make an appearance on television, even if such an appearance is wholly involuntary.

And you need help.

When the newspapers ceased being our conveyers of immediate news, the electronic media made us more vulnerable to the exposure of our fellow men. Let's face it, when a newspaper covered a story, it usually included only a picture or two of the participants in the event. But television cameras move across an entire spectrum of faces, giving momentary stardom to thousands annually, thousands who would never have been performers in their entire lifetimes.

You can ignore the frequent daily appearances you make on amateur television. In banks, stores, restaurants, public buildings, there are roving cameras watching us all. These devices are of no concern here because their audience is usually limited to an unattentive private guard, the police, the FBI or members of the security community. Professional handling of your attitudes and performance on amateur television will go largely unappreciated. Unless you are evading the authorities, a simple wave at the obvious hidden cameras as you pass will be sufficient.

Besides, I'll let you in on a secret: Most of those cameras either are not hooked up or are dummies.

What I am talking about is the common practice of the television or radio news people to interview bystanders, to call witnesses at their homes or businesses, and to include their barely edited statements on the air.

You never know these days when you or your neighbor may just pop up on the evening wrap-up, hair askew, blemishes blooming in the hot lights and opinions undraped.

Your debut becomes more plausible because of the numerous rallies, protests, upheavals, be-ins, strikes, riots and retaliations. Without the slightest intention on his part, any American might be on television any day of the week just by walking through certain neighborhoods.

Are you prepared to meet your movie-maker? Are you ready to answer the hyperactive reporter who sticks a mike in your mouth? Are you poised with the information at your disposal so that you come off to best advantage as either a participant or a bystander? Will your family be ashamed of you? Will you be the first on your block to be a has-been?

Years ago American mothers used to instruct their youngsters to wear clean underdrawers so that in case of accident the child revealed would show that he or she was the product of an interested home, an attentive mother. Today we have come so much further that one must be concerned because the truth may be evident not to just a critical few but to the whole damn community. And that's a lot of mothers.

Two very important aspects must be covered here: how to stage and participate in an event that may be covered by the media and how to act if one is involved as a bystander in an event that is covered by the media. Because you may possibly be featured in a telecast or newscast this very year, it behooves you to acquit yourself in the best tradition of show business with at least a 3 ★★★ performance.

One should know how to act if caught by the peripatetic camera or microphone today; it's a public responsibility that we all share as citizens. I am not suggesting, however, that because we have to get involved in the show business of communications we have to get involved in the situations or acts covered by the media. Certainly no one is recommending that it is your civic duty to dive into the river to save a drowning person, but it is your civic duty to be prepared to describe meaningfully how it happened.

In order to smooth your transition to this new obligatory function, let us develop some useful procedures that will increase your professionalism. Let's think of it as condensed experience, as it were.

Staging

There are observers of the media who claim that the camera and the microphone are stimuli themselves. These communications spokesmen contend that instead of the media being introduced as a result of violence, violence is introduced as a result of the media. It is impossible to achieve agreement on this contention from many of the observers whom I have questioned, but there is agreement that the media must convey what is happening and that there is attendant risk every time the equipment is introduced into a heated situation. Now, if the

observation remains valid that the media inserted into
an imbroglio results in violence, then you must be prepared to capitalize on any insertion. If you are in the
forefront of such a situation, on either side, either as a
participant or as a leader, save your best efforts for the
cameras and the mikes. Don't waste climactic violence
or your most potent rhetoric before the visiting electronics people have had a chance to set up the equipment.

If necessary, attempt to persuade the police to forestall
arrests until the media are in full possession of their
faculties. It is of little use having your top people carted
away if the folks at home are not aware of it.

Obviously timing is of the essence. No old showman is
neglectful of that precept. Even governments have
known for years about the "lunchtime principle" of
show business. Washington and New York always throw
their most impressive riots, rallies and raids at lunchtime because it is the easiest moment to get a good crowd.
The crossed fire-engine ladders on Constitution Avenue in Washington go up promptly at 11:00 A.M. as an
invitation to the government workers to join in the welcome at noon of a maharajah, a prince, a premiere or the
patrol wagon. Wall Street ticker tape flies at noon so
that the maximum audience coverage provides an impressive backdrop to the films for the evening news.

Still considering the feelings of your audience, any
premeditated efforts would preclude your having a riot
or rally during the evening rush hour. Were the camera
to comb the faces of the assembled multitude, it might
pick up only the conglomerate face of hostility, immediately costing you three or four sympathy points. It is also
imperative to remember that pamphlets and leaflets

should be given away during lunchtime when observers have time to read them dawdling on their way back to work. Dispensing such material as leaflets, etc., during the evening rush hour is useless. Your audience will simply discard the matter in favor of the evening papers for the ride home.

Be sparing in the use of shills in the crowd when the media are covering your event. Remember how the folks at home detest sham, scorning canned laughter and applause.

In anticipating trouble with the law, select your police-men carefully, mindful of the following rules: Older policemen inspire sympathy; younger policemen inspire a protective attitude on their behalf in the minds of the viewers. Attempt to select policemen who are neither too old nor too young. The best officers are those in the age group of thirty to forty who are not so pudgy that strenuous effort causes them to sneeze or breathe too heavily. Be considerate. Remember that the policemen are in the business too, and they have to make a living at it. This is the big-time for them, whereas for you it may just be an excursion into amateur theatricals.

Casting

Select your people carefully, culling out anyone with an indeterminate personality. To get the most out of your protest dollar, face up to your obligation squarely; cast people who will give you a top rating as well as a top performance. Avoid settling for people simply because they are your friends or they are hard workers. Show business requires talent—it is unavoidable—and some people are simply gifted. Understand that nothing will hurt you so much as the wrong person at the wrong time. That kind of casting will earn you laughs, and laughs deduct points in the presentation of a serious row. True, one person who gets an occasional smile as comedy relief may earn you a bonus of admiration, but the breakdown of the performance into laughter at unexpected moments will throw the timing of the entire cast hopelessly off balance.

It may be necessary to suggest that you do not load up your cast with pretty people. Pretty people are not believable and prevent your audience from developing any empathy. Pretty people make other observers jealous and frequently result in such untoward responses as "Yeah, get 'em!" and "Serves the sonofabitch right!" You don't need responses such as those indignities; they are destructive to your presentation and undo all the good your preparations may have done. There is a tendency—and it is a severe temptation—to put the best-looking people in front. Don't. Resist it and you will be more than gratified by the applause your ordinary players receive. Naturally, you will now concern yourself with whether you should have people who are less than ordinary in the forefront. Figure it out. If the audience sees painfully plain people downstage in your production, they will reason as follows: "No wonder such a person is saying this and doing that; he has a hangup about being so ugly."

Any good director will tell you where it's at today: Reality demands a look of mediocrity, of Mr. Everyman and Ms. Anywoman. Do not ignore this rule. It has cost a great many producers the forfeiture of time and money that spells f-l-o-p.

Costumes and Script

Do not denigrate the necessity for a creative costumer merely to save a few pennies. It is vital to the success of the venture that the costumer be apprised of that which has become obsolete for your kind of movement.

A graphic example of inspired costuming was that which characterized the "hardhats" of 1970. Not all of the adherents of similar philosophy wore hardhats, and not all wearers of hardhats agreed with the philosophy which was tagged by the name. But even though the coverage of any rally that was identified as "hardhat" was relatively predictable, it had dramatic impact because you knew whom you were watching and could enjoy sympathizing or dissenting without any disquieting confusion.

Now contrast the confusion resulting from the "hippie" costuming. The extensive coverage of the media brought the hippie long hair and weird clothing into such prominence that lackluster designers began to commercialize the motif. People began to wear hippie clothing or modifications of it when they had no idea in the world of conforming to the principles attributed to hippies. Hippies were made obsolete because they were unable to protect their wardrobe.

A similar situation resulted from the turnabout by the police. The police, you may recall, at one time were characterized as "pigs." The directors of various police organizations adopted the name themselves, calling themselves "pigs" with pride. It diffused the characterization completely.

Make sure that your group selects clothing and coiffures that have not been picked up by others or at least will not be assumed by government officials or people of a different persuasion from yours. Your costumer should be aware and creative so that you are always original in dress, never confusing. It does your effort no good at all to have someone interviewed as an adherent who turns out to be a Secret Service agent or an enlisted man in Army intelligence.

The script is of principal concern. You must not have one of your actors expressing one point of view and another of your people off on a tangent. Have your cast thoroughly rehearsed, totally conversant with your script so that when he or she flashes across the screen the viewer witnesses a performance that is a *tour de force*. Nothing is so destructive as desultory delivery. It makes editors and commentators angry and gives reporters an opportunity to penalize you with funny lines criticizing the performance. Don't give your critics the opening to clown around over things that good self-criticism can eliminate.

Rating System

The audience reaction to your performance is of course the most vital rating you can achieve—far more important than that of news analysts or political critics of one bent or another. But there is the age-old problem of finding *your* audience. How frequently it has been observed that no one listens to anyone but himself. Does this old saw mean that only the audience already in your corner can be expected to react favorably? Does it mean that those of the potential audience who are disposed to oppose your presentation will not watch at all? Perhaps the fundamental question is, Does any rally, protest, public demonstration do any finite good at all? To this interrogation there can be only one answer: If it makes your participants feel fulfilled, right on! It was probably Plato himself who expressed it best when he said in his magazine *Old Republic,* "The need to perform is the need to perform." This axiom was later modernized by James Cagney, who gave birth to the current "You gotta do what you gotta do."

Judging from the apparent overwhelming need to perform that is rife in the nation, broadcast presentations of confrontations should be awarded recognition commensurate with that which the professional shows receive. Consequently, I would suggest a rating system designed along the lines of that useful adjunct which has already been attached to cinematic productions. Something like the following rating system might be of aid to the viewing and listening public for public demonstrations:

GG   Generally Genial—Presentation of events suitable for all ages, all political leanings. Example: the Rose Bowl Parade.

GP   General, Parental Consent Advised—For events in which violence or dirty talk of redeeming social value may be heard. Example: sports riots, commuter breakdowns, strikes.

RR   Restricted, Right—Presentation of heavily right-wing material, parental consent advised.

RL   Restricted, Left—Presentation of heavily left-wing material, parental consent advised.

X   Xtra Bad—Presentation of material where violence, dirty talk or sex might have no redeeming social value or may be too upsetting for the psychological condition of the viewers. Adults *over* 25 years of age not permitted.

Once such ground rules are established, it would enhance the viewing enjoyment of all public upheavals and lessen the harmful effects on both children and parents. Parents could no longer blame the telly for teaching their children bad things about people, and children could prevent their parents from seeing disquieting events too. The burden of supervision and child-rearing would revert largely to the home instead of placing the blame on television.

With a rating system, students could ascertain in advance which rallies and riots they must see in order to fulfill their yearly quota, and they could avoid those with which they disagree. Parents could also know that their children were safe in the living room instead of out on some cold, dangerous street corner.

There are disadvantages inherent in such a system. There is the possibility that stations of one political inclination or other might attempt to black out some RL

or RR presentations. Stations might demand more RL
or RR events to avoid going too heavily in either direction. There is even the issue that the government might
attempt to step in and legislate control over such amateur
performances. If we are all to be included in the glamor
of show-business communications, we must be prepared
to deal with such projections on a realistic basis. Obviously ramifications such as this one demand that we
have open hearings, televised according to our new code
and rating system. Anything less would be dictatorship.

Because of the popularity of the telecasts of rallies,
protests, riots and raids, and because of the large numbers
of our fellow citizens who are starring in these presentations, there is evidence that in a system such as ours the
possibilities exist for sponsorship of such shows. Perhaps
with the improvement of the quality of such feature
presentations large firms might want to buy in as either
sponsors or actual participants in the shows. Is it too
commercial to envision the inclusion of signs in the midst
of rally posters—signs that would extol the sponsors'
products? How diverting could it be, after all, to include
among the "DOWN WITH—" signs a poster or two that said
"UP WITH MACY'S DRESSES" or some equally innocuous
plug.

Would it be more advantageous to have the sponsor
work in his product advertisements more subliminally
in such a manner as supplying uniforms for the participants with the name on the back, or have the folks
munching his product until the fight starts?

And how about the city, state and national governments? Isn't it conceivable that they also would like to
benefit by placing public-service messages on conspic-

uous areas? It would be of vast advantage to the community if, on the backs of the police uniforms, there could be embroidered such slogans as "Support Your Local Police" or "Your Taxes at Work."

Unquestionably, there is a great deal of trial and error demanded because of factors none of us has anticipated. There is the eventuality that stars would rise from among the ranks of the uniformed police in the same manner that stars have already been elevated among the radical activist groups in the country. There would undoubtedly be the logical sequence of events where one policeman, appearing frequently on camera and possessed of that blessing of star quality, would soar in the affections of the viewers. His natural gift coupled with his training would place a higher value on his services because of his talent to satisfy audience demand. Show business has perennially produced stars, and stars have produced temperament and problems. There is the danger of contract "holdouts" and rising production costs to the police department that must be foreseen.

This relatively simple problem is indicative of the labyrinth of complications which will more than likely result in our new society of show-business communications. Will star policemen have their numbers retired when they turn in their badges? Will certain groups in their encounters prove so entertaining and rewarding that they have to be rematched? Will the necessity develop for league riots and a World Series or Academy Award type of finals? The situation is not so cut and dried as one would immediately believe.

It is imperative that we discuss the plight of the average American who is inadvertently flung into the show-business situation as a performer. This is not a situation necessitating sympathy; this is a situation involving a need for preparation. How tragic, for example, to have a microphone shoved into one's face, a camera studying one's reaction, and respond as did Mrs. J. M. of Washington, D. C. Mrs. J. M. was faced with a local disturbance in her neighborhood. She stood in front of the camera, her arms full of groceries and her hair full of rollers. She was asked for her opinion of the riot and, without thinking, I'm afraid, responded, "Why don't these shitheels get the hell back where they belong?" Even with the meticulous bleeping, her reaction was hardly one that enhanced her status as a performer. She was so disturbed that she called the TV station at 2:00 A.M. in sheer frustration.

How much better for Mrs. J. M. to be prepared for such a performance with proper theatrical conditioning. In fact, how much better for all of us to observe a few simple directives with which every professional performer is acquainted. It might be well to write these notes on a separate piece of paper, have it laminated and carry it in one's pocket or purse at all times:

A. Know yourself. Know who you are and how you feel about things. This kind of introspection will allow you to have interesting and ready answers for any occasion on which you are called to pontificate. Stay alert to what is going on around you so that when you are asked, in front of an audience, "What happened?" your performance will be spotless. If you are unprepared to speak about an occurrence, shocked or inclined to be noncommittal, never say, "No comment." You will end up the legendary face on the cutting-room floor. Have a joke ready, some little tidbit which will endear you to the audience so that at least you will be included in a memorable cameo appearance.

B. *Enhance your natural attributes.* Know your good side for the camera and try to make sure that you appear at your best. Try accenting your best features; wear a wig or toupee if necessary. There is nothing to be ashamed of these days if you avail yourself of the latest cosmetic surgery. No one ever scoffed at someone who made the most of himself. And, if necessary, a few diction lessons might be of some help for the fuller realization of your capabilities.

C. *Be cool.* Breaking down in the face of a personal tragedy detracts from the situation itself. It also makes you appear, when you are unable to control yourself, as if you are attempting to steal the show. Always be in control of your emotions. And never, never try to upstage the news event which is being covered with a remark destined to show that you consider yourself, your performance or reaction more important than the main event. Nobody likes a smart-ass.

D. *Leave word of your whereabouts at all times.* This advisory is vital in case you are called for a statement and are not available. You do not want to miss your golden opportunity.

But of course the final admonition is the most important. It is reserved for those of you who may be fortunate enough in the next months to become a star performer in a news event. Perhaps you will be victimized yourself in some notable violence or you may be the glowing subject of some horrible public scandal. You may even go to jail Do not let such opportunities corrupt your dignity. Remember, the attributes that make a star are: mystery, command of the situation, and humility.

Don't overdo; don't give everything you've got on the first on-camera appearance or they will never put you on again. Be slightly mysterious without being coy. If you are physically injured, it is permissible to pause for an occasional groan or fetching wince, but do not corn it up.

Don't confess immediately to everything; humility is the true mark of the celebrated performer. Leave a little for somebody else. If you are injured, try to get off the camera or mike on your own steam. There is nothing more commendable than the American trait of self-sacrifice. If you are handcuffed or being held, look to the sky when being taken away. It's a gesture that has been popular since silent films and it never fails to bring down the house.

You know, it is conceivable that the moment you put this book down *you* may be able to use some of the information you have procured here. One never knows what the next knock on the door, the next step outside, the next telephone call, the next human being may deliver that will put you in the limelight.

In which case, we'll be seeing you!

CHAPTER THREE

Honesty
Is the Worst
Policy

Sir Francis Bacon was not all wrong when he said, "A man walking down a major thoroughfare in a large city, singing out loud to himself, is a nut. But when another man starts watching the man who is singing out loud, that's already a show." Maybe it was Herman Melville who said it.

To have a show there has to be something to watch and somebody watching. Not so long ago, and it really seems much longer than it was, TV had the viewers to entertain and the time to fill. What it lacked was programming to fill the time to entertain the viewers. There were no movies made expressly for TV. There were no reruns because there were no runs. There was no fabulous weekly treasury of pro games to build epic series for the eager fans. In that quaint yesterday, the television people decided to do something unusual. They came upon the idea of putting everybody into the act—real people, ordinary people, to entertain other ordinary, real people.

31

It may not sound very inventive to us now, but it was a time when the DuMont television network had one show where they stuck a camera out the window and read poetry to the traffic of Madison Avenue. It was called "Window on the World," and it was almost better than nothing. It was the beginning of the era of the game show and the giveaway show.

The giveaway shows, with real people, used techniques which they hoped would enhance the dramatic quality of the giveaway business. After all, they reasoned, if the viewer at home is more entertaining than the people he is viewing, goodbye. They formulated the device of using illusion to pace the shows, to make them more interesting, to achieve a more intense buildup to the climax. They graduated the excitement so that the everyday people were surrounded by an aura of such titillation that the folks at home simply could not turn off the set. And as the weeks progressed, the producers kept increasing their efforts until finally the entire land found those giveaways a barrel of laughs. There was something for everybody: little working people proving to be brilliant in science, opera and literature. There were double-dome college intellectuals spouting baseball records and boxing minutiae. It was a calculated giddiness which had the country breathless. And it resulted, this crescendo of activity, in a revolution in the public attitude toward television.

A personal note may help to explain. In one of the years prior to the Big Bust, I was a member of a typically mercurial TV panel show. The conception of the show was less than brilliant, and we panelists managed to maintain a flow of mediocrity that was consistent with the nature of the show. We were depending on the fact that Americans have big hearts and are willing to help the underdog. Perhaps we figured that when they saw us drowning in our own lack of inspiration they would reach out their hands and buy the advertised products if not out of a sense of payment for the entertainment, then out of a sense of pity.

The program had one noteworthy attribute: It was created and produced by a team of the most successful game producers ever seen in the country, the wealthy daddies of one successful game show after another. Whatever Markman and Wilson (assume these are assumed names) had ground out had been instantaneous coin returns. Their fun-amental professionalism made each one of their productions far superior to playing the games at home. They did not produce giveaway shows; their specialty was game shows, the panel-type shows.

Markman and Wilson knew what they were doing; they had it down to a remarkably effective formula. Each panel member in their stable of players had been primed with instructions, with methodology on how to milk each guest for laughs, for drama, for something that would make the game more suspenseful, more entertaining. For example, if you got the answer immediately, you didn't just blurt it out like a child in kindergarten; you toyed with the contestant, teased her, led her into the illusionary trap of thinking that you had gone past the right answer. You did something to make it a show-biz whiz. It was not which panelist won the game that counted; it was how you played the game to make it more of a fun thing that was good for having your contract option picked up.

It worked. The games, considering how simple-minded most of the premises were, were fascinating and, with one or two exceptions, were responsible for huge audiences. It was complete illusion, those multitalented stars of stage and screen using their wiles, their trade tricks, their personalities to build up the suspense and the drama to the end of each round until you were led delightedly into the next commercial. The games gave you fun, they gave you a moment away from yourself, and they gave you delightful people with whom to spend your boring hours instead of your family and friends.

Sometimes they gave the panelists something else— the answers. They did not exactly give you the answers. The director of the show would drop around to the dressing room before you entered the stage, while you were being powdered and primed to be delightful.

"I'd like to fill you in on tonight's guests. A few little pieces of information that you should know," he would say.

"Don't tell me. I don't want to know anything," I would abjure. I wasn't any more honest than anybody else, but I was not a good enough actor to feign anticipation if I had nothing to anticipate. I was, in fact, hard pressed to keep from shouting out an answer on the rare occasion when I had one. And worst of all, when they gave me information that was just information, I dawdled over it so long I used up my time interviewing the guest over some insignificant piece of background that had struck my fancy.

"Maybe you had better not give me any information at all," I finally decided to tell the director.

"I'm not giving. I'm hinting," he rejoined, as if he

were sorry that he had not taken that job offer to go to Hollywood he must have had. It was traditional even in those days, as it is today, for everyone in New York to announce that he had spurned offers to go to Hollywood because he thought the movies would go out of business. In Hollywood, it is customary to announce that you have spurned offers to go to New York because you are afraid that New York might go out of business. "Giving," he continued, "would be telling you what to ask for the answer. Hinting is dropping a little pittance of information for you to bite on that might just possibly elicit a laugh. It is my job to make sure that every panelist gets his share of laughs."

"But when you give—hint—you throw me off. As it is, I barely can remember who the sponsor is and the names of the other panelists and the guests and how you play the game. If you hint anything else I'll forget my own name and waste time guessing *that*."

"Just try to pay attention to the game and listen to the questions that the others ask. Then the hints will fall into place and you will be able to sparkle with answers." He said it as convincingly as he could, as if he almost believed it. But as he was about to leave, he stopped for a moment and began to explain the facts of life about the television games that were beginning to sprout up everywhere. "You know, you're ridiculous. Take the hints. It's for the good of the game. If it's the honesty of the game that worries you, you have no concern at all. After all, ours is purely a game show. Are we giving money away?"

He had me there. Ours was a game show and, come to think of it, Markman and Wilson never gave money away.

"But down the street," the director signified as he pointed in the direction of the next three television theaters, "down the street, my boy, they are giving away money as if they were the government. And those shows, baby, are fixed." There was a note of intrinsic wistfulness in his voice as he told me, as if he hoped that, some day, he too would be in the big-time.

There was a lesson to be learned from the program, however, the difference between illusion and delusion. It has always been acceptable for producers to give birth to shows that feature illusion—that's what it's all about. To tell the panelists to hold back, to tease even if they knew an answer immediately, was illusion; to give them the answers outright was delusion. Panel shows were not involved in fixing because their point was not money but fun, fun, fun. Except ours, which was bad, bad, bad. We were fortunate in that we were able to save ourselves from temptation, for as the summer came to an end and the leaves fell, so did we. Maybe we should have accepted the answers.

For all its fiddling with reality, the little game show was hardly comparable to the finaglings and outright larceny into which some of the giveaway shows developed. In a few years the giveaway craze had built to such a pinnacle that the games were a substantial part of the nation's weekly excitement. In order to accentuate the suspense of the ordinary people who had been elevated to temporary stardom, the producers had delved deep, going past what was illusion and propelling themselves and their contestants into delusion. The fad built and built until a disgruntled contestant blew the whistle and the entire fantastic structure came crashing down, an inverted pyramid top-heavy with its own indecencies. It brought the FCC, Congress, the courts and two police dogs. Comes the revolution.

The government, as the god of licenses, stepped in to underline the point of embarkation between the real and the surreal. Orders from the FCC were issued so that commercial producers and advertising agencies which simulated a something or other had to notate clearly that there was a simulation. Tape-recorded episodes had to be designated as prerecordings; promotion prizes when awarded had to be notated so that the public would not necessarily believe the testimonials that resulted. The government insisted on a reformation of the entire TV picture regarding programs, commercials, newscasts, recording, anything where there was a potential for any delusion and in some cases where there was the potential for illusion.

Goodbye, giveaways; hello, credibility gap. The audience had seen its delightful, dancing darling cavorting in front of the footlights and had made the mistake of following her backstage. There the audience had seen the dirty dressing rooms, the torn stockings, the padding on her front and the "Fuck You Charlie" written on the back of the scenery. The razzle dazzle of TV was so badly tarnished that you never could trust anything you saw on TV again.

That credibility gap. We did not know then that it had been established because no one had made the expression up yet. An Administration that arrived years later was responsible for the birth of the words, but the uneasy feeling about TV was already present, waiting to be exploited.

We already knew that we could no longer entirely trust TV.

When the first credibility-gap Administration began to understand the power of the medium and the more important facility of how to manage the medium, we were heading into deep and murky waters.

Omission and commission were visited upon us daily in releases to the news sources, who dutifully ground them up in the grinder of electronic news and then fed them to us. As the news became more and more painful and unacceptable, the government began to manipulate it a trifle to make it more palatable. And the manipulations were revealed as "managed news" in the broadcasts of the TV and radio newsmen. There were denials and counterdenials, and the public squirmed and cringed and wondered. It seems that Honesty had gotten a Dear John letter from the government.

The news-media bosses and their newsmen were mad as hell, charging that the government had done dirt to their gal. The government retorted that the news people were untrustworthy, making conclusions where there were no conclusions and failing to understand the complexities of running a great big democracy like ours. The issue became one of the goodies against the baddies, depending on which side you were on—the news people against the government.

And after the summer of discontent of 1968, the Administration changed and brought with it a whole new breed. The new bunch had in its employ a few television and advertising men and demographics experts, specialists of their own whom they had recruited from the media.

The new government spokesmen said, "Folks, the world isn't all that bad, is it? There are a lot of bad people, but they are not you and I. They are probably just a few outside elements who are trying to put this beloved country down."

And the news people answered, "Folks, it really isn't so good. We have riots. We have war. We have poverty. And we have some serious problems too."

The government spokesmen announced, "Don't listen to those complaining intellectual funny-faces. Those big-city guys, they're just trying to put the plain folks like us down. Things aren't really all that bad if you keep a smile on your lips and your eyes on the flag."

The newsmen kept hacking away at the nasty-looking clouds in the supposedly clear blue skies and saying, "Hurricane warnings, stormy clouds ahead and a few setbacks too."

For a rebuttal, the government spokesmen looked very ingenuous and pronounced, "Now look, folks, we don't believe in censorship, do we? Nobody does, right? But the boys in the newsrooms are certainly not behaving nicely. Now even though the media are licensed by the government, we certainly wouldn't want to censor them, would we?"

And the media jumped, "Hoo ha, did you hear that! Just by denying that they are going to censor us, they're threatening us!"

And the government seemed appalled. "We said we wouldn't censor them, didn't we, folks? Folks, didn't we say that as long as they behave themselves and stop trying to act like a bunch of New York smart-alecks, we wouldn't censor them? I mean, how can we do anything if every time we do it they're right in back of us criticizing us? If they will just be a little more considerate, they won't have a thing to worry about when they use the public air. Right, folks?"

The spokesmen were the top elected officials in the country; they owed their allegiance to the people who elected them. The newsmen were not elected by anybody; they owed their allegiance to everybody. The government spoke with authority, with power and with one point of view. The newsmen were a motley crew of thousands who had no authority, no real power and hundreds of points of view. Nobody ever hired a newsman primarily for his politics; nobody ever elected a politician for anything else.

But the Administration missed the most vulnerable point in any case against televised news, and they may have missed it for the obvious reason that it affects their case as well. We may keep coming back to it, but news on television is a show. Newsmen may deny it and tell us that nobody sits in the catbird seat and says, "Tonight we've got a really big show: four murders, three civil wars and a real-l-ly big riot in Denver!" But when it comes across the screen, it is still prepared as a show. The programs are edited for the greatest dramatic impact, paced for the most interesting and effective flow and timed according to the most interesting coverage of a story.

Everything on television is a show or a program. News on television is called a "news show" or a "news program." The newsmen, although they do not consider themselves actors, wear makeup, are selected for their ability to project a story, to possess an air of authority which they have acquired through years of rehearsal.

Even an immediate, fast-breaking (a beloved news expression) story, when it is covered on television, has the air of having a beginning, a middle and an end— just as a good play should have. It is nothing that the news personnel plan; it just evolves that way. Film should be edited to fit the requirements of time, but it is also edited for dramatic impact. Often a film clip is given more time, because of that impact, than the story merits; it simply makes a better program.

It does not mean that there lies a dire conspiracy here just waiting for its chance to pull the country down by its heels. What it does mean is that we must accommodate ourselves to the notion that television news is rich in realism but not reality. So we are back to the same gnawing doubt that permitted the government to hack away at the news people.

The reason, in Washington, that they never mentioned the fact that the news is a show is because every time they appear on television it is also a show, except that politicians are historically accorded the privilege of putting on a show; newsmen are not.

Now remember, the folks were inclined that that son-of-a-gun, that television, that never could be trusted. Those newsmen were bad apples all right; they never did bring any good news around. They were always bringing all that bad news into the house, that war and that killing and those drugs and those bad kids. You just could not trust that TV. It was the $64,000 Question all over again.

There were a few penny-ante questions that were sniffing around at the foot of the table, however. What would over 7,000 television and radio stations with thousands of news personnel have to gain by distorting the news? Would any one of the news people have to stand for re-election? When is normality, the everyday routine pursuit of the world's stable business, news? Should a facility that derives its life from the government say only niceties to protect that life? Is honesty the best policy?

The acrid odor of the threat of censorship began to pervade the air, infuriating the more free-swinging newspapers and magazines. But the electronic headliners were brought up sharply by this odor. They had smelled it before and they recognized the subtle reminder that the granting of licenses and their consequent renewal is not an automatic process. They toned down considerably.

The intention of the news people had been most laudable. There were a few on the right and a few on the left who were obviously attempting to legislate by sequestered editorials, but for the larger part of the fourth estate (or fifth, since TV had brought inflation to the size of the group) there was only the purposeful display of realism to the mass audience.

It must be suspected that that mass audience was really not interested in seeing what was happening as a result of the unpleasantness in the quasi-war in which we were semi-engaged. Any showman could have told the government that this non-war was one which most Americans would like to have seen tucked under the bed, and a bed preferably not their own. After all, with the exception of an unsuccessful John Wayne picture, where were the war pictures? Where were O'Reilly and Ginsburg and Jones and Kowalsky laughing their way through rice paddy and jungle? Where were the musicals about boot camp and the epic flyboy movies of the Air Force? Where were all the eager starlets rushing to the replacement depots of the Pacific?

O'Reilly and Ginsburg and Jones and Kowalsky may not have been appearing at the drive-ins because they were on TV every night in person. Gomer Pyle may have been in the Marines, but it was certainly not the same Marines who were fighting in the Far East. If the war was so unpopular, the show-business moguls figured, why not forget it? Why not dramatize the other events which were unfolding around the world and throughout the nation?

Good thinking! What were the "other events"? There was a verdant choice of drugs, sexual upheaval, rampant crime, newly revealed incomparable poverty, black people who were suddenly demanding a piece of the action, Russkis and Chinks who could wipe out Minneapolis in thirteen minutes, and Indians and Spanish Americans who came out of their reservations and their siestas to find that they had been getting screwed without being kissed. There were so many blossoming revolutions brewing behind the nation's insouciance that most people did not have the time to find out what insouciance meant.

They did it again. The producers of the programming that filled our eyes each night decided to put everybody into it once more. This time round, however, they decided to dramatize the problem which faced us and which came under the heading of *relevance*. Relevance filled our screen as soon as the chime sounded prime time. Lawyers and doctors coped. Teachers and police coped.

Politicians and pastors coped. Everybody was coping in
the movies and on TV. Relevance was the money word
as the Seventies dawned and yawned.

The postman rang twice for old Honesty. Since most
of the problems with which the dramatizations dealt had
no solutions, the truth of the matter was that any program that ended happily was a devaluation of the currency of the problem. In the twenty-five minutes and fifty
minutes left to programs after commercials, was there
really time to solve anything? Was it possible to end the
show on an up note? Solving an intense dilemma of life-
and-death proportions in a TV show or a movie merely
made the problem more unreal, easier for the audience
to remain uninvolved.

Television ran into the reality problem once again.
Let's say you are the writer of a weekly dramatic series.
The pay is good, the home in Hollywood Hills is splendid, you probably party with some of the biggest names in
the business. You devote yourself to your writing because
you do not want your name on the $1 map of Famous
People's Homes to be replaced by a For Sale notation.

You are a mini-god, creating people and their problems and erasing the problems by the time the final network cue chases your show off the screen. Perhaps in your
quest for relevance you do a show on the drug problem.
You write the conflict and the problem and the solution.
You cannot leave those millions of Americans from
Bakersfield to Baltimore with a sour taste in their tube.
It may be slightly simplistic in description, but you settle
the entire affair in your allotted time so that there is hope
and a smile and a tear and a satisfied sponsor.

You turn off the set and count your fee. The show

following yours is a documentary on the hopelessness of the drug problem in America, an honest appraisal of the lack of answers to the plethora of questions. You offer solutions to your dramatized relevance; honesty offers only a kick in the stomach. If *you* were entirely honest, your home would be up for sale the next option period and that big bank would unceremoniously withdraw your credit card.

What happens when that same little twenty-one-inch face tells us the true story of the day's problems, follows with a make-believe story about the same problems and then perhaps details another true recitation? The relevance becomes fuzzy, the real situation less real, and the observer who sits listening and watching the recitation becomes less and less involved.

If there is a national tendency not to believe the little face already, dramatizing the problem on the same face merely increases the prejudice.

Relevance means that whatever it is, it should relate to you. There is always something about dramatization on television that prevents it from relating to you. Perhaps it is the size of the screen, perhaps it's the fact that you can turn it off whenever you are so inclined.

Maybe it is because everything that is happening today is so incredible that the only way we can handle it is to make believe what's happening is make-believe. And everybody knows that make-believe is not honest—and it is certainly irrelevant.

CHAPTER FOUR

Radio—
the Recalcitrant
Corpse

"Harold, I want to talk to you," Mrs. Miller says to her older boy. Have to be careful, mustn't upset Harold because to upset Harold is to drive Harold away, into a cocoon, to smoking pot, to balling the dark girl with the Indian headband, the one who sports the leather dress with tassels.

"Huh, Mom?" Harold never really had much to say to his parents. What is there to say? They brought him, unasked, into the world that they were busy screwing up. They invented and used the hydrogen bomb, oppressed the blacks and robbed the Indians.

"Harold, your father and I, we were talking and wondering if you had come to any conclusion . . ." Careful, Mrs. Miller, this is a nineteen-year-old embryonic volcano. "I mean, you don't have to make up your mind this instant, but—"

"Shit, Ma, I told you already. I want to communicate.

But I don't want to talk about it. I know what you want to know and you know I know, but you act like you don't want to know that you know. I want to rap on the air."

"Harold, I know you told me that you want to be a disc jockey, but, Harold, wouldn't you be better off with a job? Maybe a profession? When you have finished studying law, tailoring, engineering, typing or veterinary, then if you want to rap, you can . . . rap." Rap on the air. Is that really a life's work? Mrs. Miller can only see this fruit of the womb with his girl, going to ask for the hand of the one he loves. Her father looks at the lad with eager interest.

"What do you do for a living, young man?" the future father-in-law asks.

"Well, I rap." Is that an aspiration for the tele-real world? What kind of a father is going to turn over what kind of a daughter to that kind of an answer? A further probe seems indicated.

"Harold," his mother starts up again, fighting the tears, "doesn't one need a kind of training for this disc jockeying? One doesn't just get on the radio and . . . and . . ." She cannot bring herself to say it again—rap.

"Nah, Ma, how hard can it be? You play a record, you talk, you do a commercial, you play a record. The records you get from the record company and the commercials come in from the advertising agencies. You get a lot of stuff for free and you are a celebrity and you make big bread. There's nothing to it, Ma."

"Harold, at least you could think of becoming a newscaster. Look at David Brinkley and Harry Reasoner. At least they wear suits."

"Ma, I just want to be a deejay on the radio," Harold says, holding his transistor radio to his ear. "Can't you let me do my thing?"

"I don't know, Harold. How can I explain to your father? I mean, what will he think of it?"

What indeed will Harold's father, the pediatric dentist, think about it? Will he think Harold is a nincompoop? Does he already think Harold is a nincompoop? Would Dr. Miller be interested in this kind of oral exercise?

Dr. Miller learned long ago that instead of being your ordinary run-of-the-mouth dentist, he had better specialize in his profession in order to generalize in his financial investments. Now he has some real estate, some savings and some friends who, by coincidence, want him to form a coalition to buy a radio station. Mr. Jules, the jeweler, told Dr. Miller, "A radio station would be funds and fun. I mean, how much do you have to know about it? You have a manager who knows something, you audit the books to skim the profit and everything else is easy. There's plenty of audience because surveys show that there are more people listening to the radio now than when it was popular. Besides, you could put Harold to work rapping."

And Dr. Miller thought, "How hard can it be?"

What happened to radio, if Harold and his father are correct? Is radio in America merely a money mill grinding out the same insipid insignificance day to day, year to year? In a word, the answer is "Well, yes." The *well* is reserved for a few exceptions throughout the nation which promise a brighter day or which reflect the actions of the remaining operators who respect the medium. The *yes* is reserved for those of you who have taken a moment to analyze what you hear from the approximately six thousand grinders every day.

The radio industry begat the TV industry. And the TV industry needed a great deal of nursing, so it drew its attendants from the radio industry. In the beginning, the personnel were interchangeable, radio to TV, TV to radio. And the years passed and TV flourished and the people knew the TV industry. And the multitudes paid little attention to the radio and the movies and the newspapers.

And the radio was dead and it was buried. And Rock was placed over its head to mark where it was laid. And on the third day, give or take a decade, radio rose up again and spurted money from its ghoulish mouth and it was resurrected.

But it had been through the fires of hell and it was not the same radio that had been buried. It was a hard-nosed, brassy, money-grubbing harlot in its new life. And it had found its place: background to the other clatter in America, polluter of the air, adding a steady rhythm of din and commercial carnivalia to the land. The creative people who were in radio had emigrated to the New World of Television, where the streets were paved with bullion and edged with the excitement and glamor which accompanies being Number One.

The newborns, the creative people just arriving into the bright world of broadcasting, headed for television. Even if they started in radio, they kept looking for the little red light on the cameras. Upon consideration, they were correct in their inclinations because the only inclination for radio was a downward one.

Radio had become a retail store. There were supermarkets and there were corner groceries, but the radio stations had allowed themselves to be converted from showplaces to doughplaces.

Radio is there to sell products, not incidentally but primarily. Radio gives away little premiums to get you into the store: a little music, a little service, a little news, but just enough to entice the listener to pick up the economy size or the six-pack.

With the conversion to the hard-money system of radio was born the most destructive influence in the broadcasting field. The name of the culprit is one with which most ordinary, decent Americans are familiar. Demographics. The definition of the word as listed in the newer, hipper dictionaries would have you believe that this word means the study of social statistics—e.g., births, deaths, ages, income, breakdown of people of certain ages of certain income, breakdown of people of certain ages of certain income of certain color, breakdown of people of certain ages of certain color of certain buying habits. Breakdown of people as people and reassembly as numbers.

This is how we all seem to have become fellow numbers in the same club. Demographics is the legitimate child of the bastard rating systems, those rickety suppositions which were originated to give the sponsors a buying guide to listening audiences. When Mr. Burton Birdseed had a new jingle created to sell his birdseed—"Open your beak for birdseed and you'll have a better beak. A better beak and downier down, you'll have the strongest bird in town!"—when Mr. Birdseed had that jingle composed, he wanted the greatest number of bird fondlers pampering their birds that he could find for his dollar.

He wanted the cost of each thousand people listening to be as low as possible. The only way that he could ascertain just how many people were available for his birdseed was through the use of the rating system, which gave an approximation of the size of the audience of each station.

Birdseed's advertising agency analyzed the ratings and told Birdseed where he could stick his money, his mouth and his birdseed. There remained only one problem— besides Mr. B.'s recurring heartburn and his blond secretary.

The rating systems, on which he was forced to pin his money, were resplendent with inaccuracies as a way of life and were often forced to rely on imagination. Some of the surveys used telephones (the Call and Query the Quarry Method), some of the surveys used the diary method (the Write Down Anything to Fill Up the Page Way).

There were enormous complications, such as the lack of adequate sample size, the resistance of a subject to admit what he was really, really listening to, and the confusion resulting from the maelstrom of AM, FM and TV signals pulsating through the blue. What could a guinea pig remember?

Let us take, for example, an excerpt from a transcript of a telephone call to the subject of a rating survey:

INTERVIEWER: Hello, this is Pernicious Investigating Service calling. May I ask you if you are listening to the radio, please?

SUBJECT: Hello. What? Wait a minute, will ya. . . . (Talking to someone else away from the telephone) Turn off the TV,

	will ya! I can't hear. (Returns to phone) Now, whatya want?
INTERVIEWER:	This is a radio rating service calling. Are you listening to the radio, please?
SUBJECT:	Who wants to know? Sam, is this you, you crazy bastard! Are you kidding around again?
INTERVIEWER:	No. No, this is an actual radio—
SUBJECT:	What's the prize?
INTERVIEWER:	Well, there is no prize, but we feel that you are unquestionably helping the radio and the advertising industries to give more reliable, finer service and better programs to the listener.
SUBJECT:	How much is the jackpot?
INTERVIEWER:	There is no prize.
SUBJECT:	Sure, sure for this shit you call me, but for the prizes—
INTERVIEWER:	Madam, just a moment, won't you please give me a brief answer to a few questions?
SUBJECT:	Go ahead, I'll give you an answer all right.
INTERVIEWER:	What is your favorite station?
SUBJECT:	What's that classical-music station?
INTERVIEWER:	WXNY?
SUBJECT:	Yeah, yeah.
INTERVIEWER:	What is your favorite program from six A.M. to seven A.M.?
SUBJECT:	News, you know, the all-news station.
INTERVIEWER:	WXEX, so that most of the day—
SUBJECT:	Most of the day? All day I listen to the

news on the news station and the music on the classical station, that's all I ever listen to.

INTERVIEWER: Well, thank you very much. You don't realize how far this goes toward improv—

SUBJECT: You don't work for that MediaStudia station, the one with Jack Mouth, do you?

INTERVIEWER: No, this is an independent survey. You probably mean KGASS.

SUBJECT: Yeah, that's the one. Tell Jack Mouth that he is full of it and that he talks too much between records. And his records ain't no good either. And he waits too long to give the race results.

INTERVIEWER: But, Madam—

SUBJECT: Look, don't argue! I know what I'm talking about. I listen to that station all day long.

From intensive work done by those superb surveyors, Professors Masters and Johnson, it has been ascertained that people approached by surveyors in person tend to give the following misleading information:

63 percent of those questioned attempt to give answers that they surmise the surveyors want to hear.

9 percent of those interrogated name stations and programs that they listen to, although they do not own radios.

22 percent of those approached maintain that they listen only to cultural improvement shows.

3 percent are not at home and have the milk, the mail, the papers and the surveys taken in by the neighbors.

1 percent say that, although they do not agree with everything he says, Senator Joe McCarthy is doing a great job in Washington.

1 percent sic dogs on the surveyors, forcing the surveyors to make up the answers.

.5 percent expose themselves to the female surveyors.

.5 percent of the female subjects are witches and the surveyors disappear.

The radio stations and Mr. Birdseed learned to live with the filigree of fantasy because there was no alternative. An advertising agency wanted numbers as a criterion for spending money allotted to radio advertising. They needed the numbers for a valid reason, one which makes a great deal of cents when analyzed.

After a wondrous laying-on of pressure, the agency has been apportioned $2.5 million by Birdseed to spend for advertising—15 percent of which they receive as the agency fee. The ad agency has determined that it would be wise to spend $2 million on television, $.5 million on radio. It's possible.

It is an absolute breeze to spend $2 million in TV land because of the cosmic prices for TV time, local and national network. Add to this shock the cost of producing television commercials which must have the look of professionalism instead of that of a stag film.

The expense of producing radio commercials is infinitesimal compared to the cost of producing an imaginative television commercial. Imaginative radio commercials have largely been confined, along with the most imaginative radio, to that radio cemetery where rests the dry cell,

the vacuum tube, the radio dramatization and the fault-
less diction of the old stentorian announcers. More about
commercials later on. At this time we must hurry and
meet the time buyers.

The advertising-agency time buyer, usually a buxom
pussycat of twenty-two, can spend $2 million for airtime
before she goes to lunch, provided that her previous
night's encounter has not been so strenuous that it diverts
her morning after.

The overhead on airtime expenditure so far is only our
buxom baby doll with her salary of $12,000, and that is
her Christmas bonus, pension and retirement plan all
rolled into one. Anything else the agency throws in is
infamous padding, and we have already resolved that
our buyer doesn't need *that*.

But to spend $500,000 on radio airtime is a major
adventure. There is really no radio network left except
a few condescending news services left over from primor-
dial days, so the half million has to be sprinkled in
dribs and drabs throughout the vast coterie of local stations. Research—often research is another word for fudg-
ing the demographics—has to be accomplished, analyses
of the various types of radio stations: middle of the road,
country and western, teentime, all talk, all black, ethnic.
Then when the holes in which to place the pegs have
been calculated, it becomes obvious that because the
price of radio airtime is so inexpensive compared to that
of television, one needs a staff to compute where to ap-
portion the money.

Now we have to have more than one buxom twenty-
two-year-old; we need three buxom young ladies, one
long, lean sophisticated type, two secretaries, one super-

visor and a partridge in a pear tree. No $12,000 overhead
this; let's settle for $96,000—and there is a lot less fee
to draw from, 15 percent of a half million compared to
TV's 15 percent of $2 million. It hardly pays our ad
agency to open its gold-encrusted, figurine-embellished,
insulated doors for the radio business.

More ratings and calculations; less problem selecting
commercials from the endless sea of radio availabilities.
Our agency time buyers need a profile of the numbers
of listeners so that they can figure the lowest cost to buy
each thousand of them. When the agency buys time for
commercials in communities where they have no listening post, they are really buying blind. They must know
what is going on out there in remote radioland.

Illustration: One of the small conglomerates which
owned radio stations had none in New York. The little
group did have stations in other parts of the country
which received delightful amounts of money from New
York advertising agencies. In a stroke of what they
thought was gross good luck, the group was able to buy
a radio outlet in New York and revamp it to conform
to the format of its other, successful as Las Vegas, stations.

"Now," the owners exulted, "the agencies can hear
our successful beauty sounds right in their own smoggy
backyards!"

When the agencies in smug, smoggy New York heard
the station, when they heard the kind of badness into
which their commercials were being insinuated, they
ripped their commercials off the New York station as
well as the ones in the hinterlands.

Within two or three months the little group had converted their New York station to a Spanish-language station. The agency-type people may be *recherché* and suave and all things beautiful, but they at least will not wait around for consecutive translation. Obliviousness quickly reinserted itself and commercials flowed back.

The radio stations are anxious to help the advertiser, of course.

Now, at last, years in the making, a system that allows a station the certain determination of its position in town. "WXXX Number One in Town!" You see the advertisements everywhere, on buses, in papers, in magazines. A real aid to the advertiser, through demographics.

Demographics, a refinement of the ratings, introduces science into the equation, breaks down the audience into numbers and allows the radio stations to issue sufficient dialectics to snow any prospective time buyer. How many men, how many women, how many teens, how many chickens in every pot. Come with me, time buyer, and I will show you why, without our WXXX, your client is a hermit. The radio stations have it figured so that everyone can be classified and targeted for the Birdseeds of America.

But it is simply not so simple as all that. Evidence follows. Statement by Leo Lie, sales manager of radio station K123 in San Francisco: "Listen, when you put your birdseed on our air, you are getting the *number one* audience. We got more eighteen-to-forty-five year-olds than anybody else—Number One. You want to sell the bastards birdseed? Sell it on K123 because our audience is Number One for the kind of people who buy your products. Whatya want teenyboppers for? They're too busy playin' with their birds to be playin' with their birds."

Same city, different approach by Salesman Simple, sales manager of radio station K234: "Number One? I could show you the demos [demographics] we got the *Number One* audience from thirty-five to fifty-five— the bird lovers."

Same lovely city, desperation time. Mark Time, sales manager of KFMFM (FM station) : "Man, they're selling you tickets! Are you out of your bird? We got it all —we got Number One from 6:30 P.M. to 7:15 P.M.— nobody can touch us. Number One!"—now he whispers —"with people with red hair and green eyes who have had pre-marital intercourse in dirigibles."

Victory is for the most creative manipulator of the figures because it is he who can make those little digits do anything he wants them to do or needs them to do to sell his air.

There is another fault, besides the manipulation of the blessed figures, that makes the demographics a poor bellwether. The demographics can never take cognizance of the variables in humanity. They really can only generalize. If you are eighteen, you are the same as all other eighteen-year-olds in the nation. If you are forty-five, you are all forty-five-year-olds. If you are fifty-five, forget it; you're out of it.

The audience was researched until it had lost any resemblance to the emotional, empirical, fickle, unpredictable amoeba that it was. It became numerical, categorical, computable. Where was that fun-loving gypsy group of swingers of all ages? That's not shown in the demos. Where was that conservative, old-fashioned cross-section of sixteen to 106—that's not in the demos. Where was that filthy-minded, voyeur-prone, dirty-mouth element that lurks in all of us?

It was the same kind of mistake that statisticians always make when they statistish. The silent majority this morning may well be an entirely different group of people by the time tonight's newscasts are presented.

Such probing and prying into the nether recesses of humanity usually produce fallacious conclusions. When you feed aberrations into the computer to be multiplied endlessly, to have conclusion upon conclusion built upon the quicksand of mistakes, you arrive at that basic computer law written in the golden scroll: In the computer when you stick in half-truths, you take out whole lies.

Demographics is designed purely for the salesmen to grab and sell the audience to a sponsor. That audience will be analyzed, divided, shared, stolen and sold. Radio is not an art form; it's a business, and as a business it is too frequently run entirely by businessmen without the proper consideration for the entertainment, the enlightenment, the satisfaction of the audience.

The advertising is not superimposed on the programming; the programming is squeezed between the advertising.

Radio programs are rarely placed on the air on a basis of good programming for the sake of the audience. There is no one there to sanction or edit the creative, the innovative. Most of the executive force having been raised from the commercial ranks, their orientation is numerical and fiscal, not inventive or show business. When radio was abandoned with the advent of television, the

market for creativity disappeared and the creative people learned to go elsewhere: to the films, to the recording industry, to theater, to TV or to honest jobs in their
fathers' businesses.

There was a tender moment when it seemed that FM
(frequency modulation) stations might be able to
wrestle radio back to an eminence. FM stations have been
around a great many years; they were introduced con-
currently with television in the dim dead 1940s. But
where television grew to be a giant, FM remained a
stunted dwarf.

The FM signal, it was claimed, was static-proof, brilliant in its high fidelity, the radio of the future. What
radio of the future when this entertainment-crazy country was completely captivated by the television of the
present? So FM went slinking away, its potential drag-
ging behind it down the path of obscurity. Who needed
a new radio when television was here? And besides, the
sound portion of TV was FM radio. Wasn't that recognition enough?

For thirty years FM radio kept threatening to replace
old AM. The ingenious inventor, Dr. Edwin Armstring,
ended his life, embittered and frustrated that his creation was never to achieve significance.

Most of the stations loped along, simply duplicating
whatever the AM counterpart was doing, uninventive,
inexpensive, unproductive. FM had the potential for
broadcasting stereo from the beginning, and even the
introduction of stereo records persuaded no great leap
forward for the electronic underdog. The FMers threw
on stereo records with the same enthusiasm as they did
everything else, none whatsoever. If filthy stories on rec-

ords would have been the innovation, they would have broadcast filthy stories—anything, anything cheap to fill up the time.

Finally, two things which came completely out of left field or right field, depending on the political stance you enjoy, broke the thirty-year lethargy of FM. In one of its unpredictable swings to the right or left, the Federal Communications Commission—the overseer of all things electronic—decreed that FM stations in large cities should not be just the hi-fi twin of their AM stations. It was ordered that the FM stations broadcast their own programming at least 50 percent of the time instead of just carrying the same programs as their AM big brothers. The decree applied only to metropoli that were larger than 100,000 souls.

Frankly, who gave a damn? Who was going to listen to FM anyway? FM, that underdog, that neglected, alienated medium, who in the world was going to nurse the poor foundling until it could stand up alongside its brother, until it could fulfill its prophecy and be the New Radio?

Who? The kids, the alienated, the underdogs who felt neglected in the Sixties, they were attracted to it. It worked out nicely because the only place a station owner could, in clear commercial conscience, give a newcomer a break was in the FM division. And the kids brought young listeners to the medium. Practically non-commercial, the kids and FM spent the Sixties growing up together.

For a brief while it began to appear as if this young, experimental, populous communications phenomenon might realistically be the New Radio. There was audience, there was excitement, there were few commercials. FM had become exactly what the FCC had intended it should become, a source of additional radio stations. But the FCC was not paying for the new stations.

When management walked through the blue smoke of incense in the lobby and found excitement and audience lurking in the mossy fields of FM, they hurriedly called for reinforcements on the part of the sales departments. The salesmen retreated into phone booths, slipped on their Young America jump suits and went bounding out, seeking demographics so they could sell the airtime.

The results: Instead of FM introducing the new, the innovative, becoming a hot new radio, the demographic-lovers seized the audience, analyzed it and loaded the pink young ears with commercials. The FM commercial departments froze the FM stations into their new molds with the gleeful advice, "Don't change a thing. You must be doing something right!" Competitively, the AM stations adopted some of the new FM techniques—progressive music, young voices—but they missed the fundamental difference the FM broadcasters had introduced. They missed the innovation, the experimentation.

With the FMers now frozen, the AMers already frozen, creativity, that flimsy will-o'-the-wisp, jumped out of the window and committed suicide.

Education stations, a few non-commercial, listener-supported stations attempt to originate ear-bending, unique listening. If you twirl the dial you will hear such stations, their distraught voices begging for funds to stay alive to keep trying and experimenting. "But why," Casanova once asked, "should I have to pay for something that I have been accustomed to getting for free?" And the radio audience probably feels the same way.

Collegiate stations which should be another fount for the development in the arts of communication may be experimental and developmental, but unfortunately they are never inclined to study the realities of the commercial operation, the wedding of the creative and the commercial. Their students come to the marriage bed, virginal, untaught and intellectually puritanical. Furthermore, with the troubles the universities have had in the past few years, they are not about to risk too much experimentation in a mass medium which could excite their inhabitants to further insurrection.

Why, then, do Harold and his father, the dentist, still want to get into radio? Why has radio lived when it has been dead for these two decades?

Of all mass communications media, radio is the most personal; it's all in your head. It is a one-to-one medium. When that speaker, that singer, that newsman appears, he appears to you alone. His expressions, his innuendoes, his passion, his sports jacket are visible and viable only to your imagination. Imagination is the basis of radio; imagination has nothing to do with what appears on your TV screen.

Charles de Gaulle, in his final years in the French presidency, used radio exclusively when he needed a motivational force, when he needed persuasive clout. On the radio, the voice was de Gaulle; he was the *grand* Charles; the steel had not been corroded by age. But on TV you did not hear the clarion call to save the *République;* you saw only a worn-out old warhorse.

De Gaulle knew the value of a medium which can

harness the imagination, and imagination is the single attribute most lacking in the people who operate radio stations in America today. It takes imagination to capture the imagination.

Everybody cannot own and operate a radio station. Even everybody who can afford to do so cannot operate a radio station. The old habits established by the listeners of the past have been discarded by the sons and daughters of the fathers and mothers.

Stations which have not maintained their positions have floundered and changed, hoping to find that rating-getting formula which will make their million for them. But it takes guts, unpredictability, personal security, insanity to go out on the limb to see if you can find what it is that the people want or need. And after all, who cares about the people when it is the numbers you want?

Assume for a miraculous moment our Dr. Miller, the dentist, had gotten his friends to coalesce and indeed buy a radio station. Representing the investors, Dr. Miller would have an encounter with the station manager and the program director in an earnest effort to best determine the direction of the new toy.

The problem would be to settle on a "formula" to procure the numbers and thus procure the sponsors. All radio stations are constructed along one formula or another. The formulae begin at the extreme left with "acid rock music"—the radio version of a high—extend all the way over through middle of the road, ethnic, news, over to the far right, the "good music" station, which is a blend of classical music and show tunes—a blend which yields a small but loyal group of esoteric listeners who count their change.

The most successful stations would provide Doc, and anyone else who listens, with a mind-dulling repetition of the hits. The only experimentation he would encounter would be in the unsuccessful station, the one still desperately seeking a formula with which to become commercially successful.

For as a station acquires audience, it acquires commercials. As a station acquires commercials, it acquires caution. The paradox exists that a wildly inventive station, AM or FM, is only as creative as its sustaining time.

As was sagely formulated by one of our leading communications thinkers—I believe it was me—more audience, more commercials; many, many commercials, less audience.

So far, music remains one of the main reasons for radio's life after death, but there are other formulae which our dentist-owner might explore, the variations of talk on the air. Talk radio formulae are not so diverse: all-news radio, interviews and telephone talk shows.

The all-news station, I maintain, is not a radio station; it is a service station. It lives only in the largest cities because in a town where the biggest thing that happens all week is the arrival of Saturday night, all news is all bore. The problem with all-news is that the audience can be expected to change every fifteen or twenty minutes, the principle being that the news must be available almost on demand. If our dentist, worried about excessive turnover of the audience, loads the station up with features, opinions, knickkacks and specialty items like a newspaper, he risks the listener's turning the page. That listener wants the news.

The talk-interview station formula is as interesting as

the guests it presents, but if our owner-dentist fills the time with anything too specific, too parochial, he risks running off the other listeners. And controversy? It is essential but it does alienate sponsors. Because of topical problems, stations dealing in controversy often find themselves forced into a mold of the daily discussion of the same three or four subjects. The result is that most of the talk stations that concentrate on interviews end up with a large serving of white bread, untoasted, unenhanced and unenriched.

How about call-up radio, the kind of radio often known in the trade as "hate radio"? Hate radio is generated hate where the MC (Master of Controversy) is a master of incitement (MI?), an agitator with the avowed purpose of getting one side to call in and excoriate the other. It can be manipulated as well by using highly provocative guests who are good for a few blown fuses. The pattern evolved is (a) start trouble, (b) let the audience get involved, (c) fan the flames, (d) cool them before they scare off the sponsors. It's a good formula for brief episodes of impressive ratings.

It is amazing how quickly the audience becomes aware that the hate, the jabs to the sensitivities are really feints. In a brief span they begin to see through the pattern of kook calls and stimulated hostility and they ripple away, leaving the owner the poor fish in his polluted little pond.

Operating a radio station should be a full-time endeavor, something you love to do almost as much as sex. With sex, if you're careful, you can have a loving affair with fond memories. But with a radio station, careful or not, you may find that a chance encounter leaves you with a great many bills, an unwanted baby, a hostile public and the government looking into your boudoir.

Maybe Dr. Miller can work out his desires in the fulfillment of those of his son, Harold.

Harold, you still want to get into radio? Do you hear those blithe, breezy, bull-throwing voices telling you the big ones in Burlington, giving you the weather in their with-it utterances fluid with sex? Is that what you want, Harold, to be a star where nobody can get at you but you can get at everybody else?

The bright lights, the big names, stardom with anonymity, girls, boys, cars, cameras, stereos, money. A deejay, a radio person, learn it in six weeks, or study it in a hundred colleges and get your Bachelor of Fine Arts of Broadcasting degree! Go, Harold, go!

Before you go, Harold, consider the business aspects of working the radio supermarket. There is not a radiostation operator in the country who is looking for you, your personality and the gifts you are willing to bring. What they are really looking for is someone to accomplish the immediate disposition of all that time that sits around between the records. Unless you have some system, some scheme, some way to make your dynamism bring in the bucks, they are not interested in developing your career.

There are radio stations in the United States that automatically cut off the microphone after the announcer has spoken twenty seconds of non-commercial words. There are radio stations in the United States that do not have a human being on the premises for twenty-four hours at a time while a tape automaton plays the hits and sells the groceries. If a Harold had talent, most of the radio-station operators of the nation would not know what to do with him.

The radio performer of the future is not to be a performer at all, as we have come to know and love/hate the term. He will be a "separator," a slash between one piece of recorded business and the next. An endless tomorrow of repeating what was said on a not very memorable yesterday.

The exception is news. The sweep of television left in its wake the destruction of radio networkdom with the sole exception of news networks. Otherwise, the demise of the radio networks liberated all of the stations and established equality; all stations are forced to fill the bulk of their operating time themselves. News fills time; it can be sold and it is the best thing radio does.

When something happens, you get it first on radio— with some stations you get it worst on radio too, but we're asking for improvement, not perfection. To the Harolds of the world we say: You may not get to sleep with your latest singing group, but as a news something or other you are performing a function that is meaningful and necessary.

The problem for the aspiring radio candidate is that the equality of stations has erased the significance of "big-time" in radioland. The lack of imagination in small cities is as well developed as that in New York, Los Angeles and Chicago.

Although the possibility exists that there is more money to be made in larger cities, there is also the corollary that there is more to be spent. The desirability rests in the importance the aspirant places on extracurricular activities. Commercials, film narration, industrial shows, films are in the two coastal big cities. Romantic extra-curricular activities are prevalent everywhere, but that's uncovered in all the other books.

There are things to be done to radio before it is too late, although it may be too late already. Even if we decided that radio's proper role is primarily the broad-cast of news and music, how can we arrive at the best music and news broadcasting possible? How do we bring back radio from its screaming cacophonous flight into audible garbage?

Suppose we decided that it should be a prerequisite of its license that no station can derive 100 percent of its music from canned, commercial discs, that it would be required to provide either some live music or music taped at performances. Suppose we decided that a license was contingent on at least one third of a station's pro-gramming being live or at least taped from live perform-ances, talk discussion, dramatics, whatever.

The FCC would not tell the stations what to broadcast; the stations would have to discover what the people wanted. Create? Experiment? What a period of shifting and evading and screaming to envision before the new ideas start to flow! What a wealth of Harold Millers to be discovered, rejected, refined and elevated! What a new era when radio becomes a medium for listening rather than background! What a craziness to suppose such a revolution!

The increased cost of better programming offers too many possibilities of bankruptcies in too many places where pressure can be exerted to maintain the *status quo*. Too many elected officials own pieces of radio sta-tions to allow hope for legislative interest in the improvement of the medium. And, of course, an invitation for government to set higher standards always has the intrinsic danger of too much government control.

It is necessary that more local stations be local voices, that they stick their microphones into legislative and judicial business that is everybody's business. And it is necessary that we ask more stations to take sides and help sponsors realize that sponsorship isn't censorship— that sponsoring the word doesn't make it a word from the sponsor.

CHAPTER FIVE

How to Get
into the Act
and Get Rich
Overnight

It looks easy. The people are certainly not great actors. You know that they don't seem any more beautiful, talented, charming, competent, gifted, artistic, articulate, any younger, older, more interesting than you.

You've heard that they're making a fortune, that there are residual payments that go on interminably. There certainly doesn't seem to be any particular skill or trick to saying the things they say.

So why aren't you making TV commercials? Everybody else seems to be. If you look at the characters in the commercials, they are frequently people just like you and me; they are even identified as Mr. or Mrs. SoandSo of Split Rock, Maine, or some town near yours. Just ordinary, plain Americans. Why not you? Why not me?

You came to the right person. I have been doing TV commercials for years, on the screen and appearing as the voice off screen, the "voice-over" as it is called. I am willing to share your enthusiasm and my experience.

Stick with me, baby, and perhaps I can make you a star.

All you have to do is win an audition. The audition is the process where the people who are responsible for the manufacture of the commercial select the actors for the roles. It is the point where they look and listen and then say, "Get me that person; she'll be great for the dirty-sink lady," or "Get him! He'll be the guy who needs the deodorant."

Once we get you through the audition you'll be on your way to the top—or at least to obscurity and fortune. When you get too famous, too well known in the commercials, you become a detriment. You become stronger than the mouthwash, more unforgettable than the hemorrhoid suppository. If we can just keep you slightly impressive, yet sufficiently mediocre, with just a *soupçon* of believability, you may have a great future in commercials.

Or none at all.

Commercials run in cycles; when reality is in, everybody seems to be using real people with their names written across the bottom of the screen. When dreamy, esoteric, fanciful photography is the rage, everything from colas to foot powder becomes a fantasia of color and applied surrealism. When stage and movie stars are hot, you and I will have to sweat out the phase till they come seeking anonymity again.

Commercial costs for television have no limit. They can be budgeted at the same levels as low-budget movies —a quarter of a million dollars, for example. I participated in one cigarette commercial that was budgeted at $75,000 and never even found its way to the air.

Of course since you're new in the game, you may need an agent. The production centers—New York, Los Angeles, Chicago, Miami—are full of agents, people whose sole occupation is to hawk actors and actresses for commercials. With an agent submitting your picture or a tape of your voice—or even sending the real you in for an audition—you may bystep several months or years of making the rounds of the advertising agencies, trying to be discovered on your own.

Unfortunately, the agents are inclined to sell who is selling. Newcomers with no experience are a difficult sale, so your new agent may neglect you and neglect you. And neglect you. And never sell you at all because you are not hot as are some of his more experienced clients. Perhaps it would be more advantageous to wait until you are famous and rich, or busy, before you get your agent. But when you are rich and famous and busy, why do you need an agent? To turn down work, silly.

Perhaps you had better get the agent now. This way, when you make the rounds of the casting offices of the ad agencies, you can leave the name of your agent. Then when you walk in and they are looking for you, you can tell them to call your agent to get in touch with you.

If you achieve the heights where you become too popular, too expensive, too well known, then the casting offices will be inclined to call up and get someone who looks and sounds like you. Where, you ask haughtily, will they get someone who looks and sounds like you? From your agent.

The casting offices are the procurement sections of the advertising agencies' creative departments. The creative departments contain the writers, the art directors, the people whose ideas must be implemented to produce the final dramas which sell everybody anything.

With the current wave of commercials we have achieved the Everyman commercial type, and perhaps we should ask ourselves the question, Are you Everyman? Are you really unobtrusive enough to be representatively unobtrusive? You may need instructions from the resident experts who are berthed in New York, Los Angeles, Dallas, Miami and Chicago who can give you the excellent instructions in mediocrity so that you are everything you should be—that is, nobody in particular and yet identifiable as someone we all might know.

In compliance with the new demands for minority representation, if you are black, are you sure you are not too light or too black? If you are Oriental, you must make certain that you are generally Oriental, without being too specifically Chinese, Japanese or Philippine. If you are going to represent a European, try to ascertain that your accent is pleasantly indefinable. The agencies can always procure American dialecticians to portray specifics—French, Italian, German, Spanish—so that a cross between Hungarian and Portuguese is probably unassailable.

Dramatic training will probably be an assured liability for your commercial career, because the commercials world may look real, but it is a land of sell. The essence of that statement is that people in commercials accent the words that sell the product, not the logical emotional words to effect a dramatic coup.

If you were to rush into your neighbor's kitchen in a commercial you would scream, "Look out! There's a *white* tornado." Emphasis on the word "white" because you are selling a cleaning product. In real life, or a life-like drama, a tornado is eloquence enough to bear accenting. In the commercial, the tornado can go screw itself into the ground.

You don't have a cold, you have a *virus* cold. Your thirst is not quenched with a drink; it demands *the real thing*.

So much for dramatic training.

Television commercials are unimpeachably honest. They are the closest thing in television to a purposeful reality. They are there to sell. If they amuse and do not sell, they are worthless. If they win a thousand awards and do not move the products, they are a failure. They are the one area of television which tells you their essential truth: They are there to sell you something.

We are ready for the big assault. We are going to make you as memorable as Nagging Backache, Irregularity, Drab Lifeless Hair, Feminine Cleanliness.

Good news! The advertising agency has put out a call for your type. It is only one line of dialogue for the Bird-seed account: "Now my bird is ready whenever I am!" One line, but it is a beginning.

We appear at the casting office of the advertising agency. I have to leave you here. You are on your own. Go get 'em, Tiger!

The casting offices vary from one ad agency to another, depending on the image the agency has of itself. An agency which fancies itself as a highly creative one might maintain the impression right down to the casting offices, although casting areas are vehicles of expenditure, not income. Actors and actresses do not bring in the money;

they cause it to flow out and there is no need to foment an impression for them.

An agency which is involved in merchandising efficiency or economy quick sales will not waste funds on elaborately embellishing its production areas. On the other hand, sometimes when there have been a few good years, they have been good years right down to the softness of the toilet tissues in the john.

Be prepared for the fact that there will be other aspirants in the casting office; the place may be crowded with hopefuls for your commercial and others. You may see every young actor and actress from Broadway, even a few established stars. Rest assured that television faces will be plentiful; a commercial may not mean a fortune, but it pays somewhat better than unemployment insurance. Ask one of the actors; he'll tell you.

"Look, kid, there's a lot of competition for the buck in this game. Why, a great commercial that runs for a full thirteen weeks can bring you as much as a thousand dollars."

"A thousand dollars. That's what you make for a commercial that runs for three months?" you ask.

"Look, Mac, that's a find. One guy I know had a really big one and made three thousand dollars from one commercial in thirteen weeks. Three grand for one spot. That's a real breakthrough."

You press. "How much did he make for the whole year?"

"Three grand."

You pick up your commercial script from the receptionist. She may even give you a story board to study. The story board is a series of sketches, in sequence, which will show you the idea of the commercial as the creative people have envisioned it. You must look at your line of dialogue to search the motivation, to get into the character, to understand what it is that will make the audition panel want *you,* make them say, "That's the one."

You feel a need to test your reading of the line in that busy reception room, so you face the wall and murmur it into the graffiti. After all, what laughs if the other people were to catch the spectacle of you, the beginner, reading aloud the one little line, "Now my bird is ready whenever I am."

Suddenly your concentration is broken by a steady humming, the combined sounds of the other people in the room, a murmur as they run through their scripts, a chant as they intone the meaningful words. The voices caressing, cajoling, pleading, romancing, laughing, each voice reciting the line in a manner peculiar to his style. Ninety people with their one-line birds ready.

You slide over to a man seated on one of the twelve plastic sofas. "Is this bunch all for the same audition?" you ask the veteran.

The man looks up with a good-natured smile for the novice. "Screw off, kid. It's every man for himself. It's kill or be killed. This is my fourteenth audition this week and I haven't won one of them."

Be careful. This vet may tear your script into a thousand pieces.

Suddenly an avalanche of babies descends on the waiting room. You are pushed into a corner by an angelic three-year-old who knees you in the ankle. The mother seizes you by the neck with her two powerful hands. "Leave my kid alone, you rotten bastard. That's the trouble with you greedy actors. You ain't got no class, steal a line from a child, a little child. Pervert!" The stage mother gives you a knee in the crotch and moves on with her baby toward stardom. But don't fret, the little ones are not in competition with you; they are being presented for a film commercial, a new dydee product made of plastic that enables Mommy to save her child's effluvia so that ultimately it can be bronzed.

While you attempt to continue absorbing your information, blocking out the noise of the tiny tots screaming and fighting across the room, three Great Danes are introduced into the waiting room. The dogs are auditionees—don't worry, it's not for your commercial—for a pet-food outing. Try to retain the aura of detached tolerance. Remember you can't begrudge a dog a few bones to set aside for his dog days.

Suddenly it is you whose name is being called in the waiting room. *They* are going to listen and look at you. *They* are going to consider you for a commercial. Your instructions are to proceed toward Audition Room Three through a lengthy corridor lined with cubicles.

Each cubicle is an office for another agency luminary, his assignments designated by the successful ads posted on the wall. In one of the cubicles the luminary himself may be hanging on the wall; success is not easily won in the ad game.

Your mind races with questions, so you give it problems to solve, to calm you down. You consider things such as whether you should ask for name credit on the commercial, whether you should make suggestions about the camera direction and production ideas.

Audition Room Three is in actuality a miniature

studio. It has a videotape camera and microphones. There is a control booth jammed full of people. An attractive young person dressed in a jump suit meets you in the door of the audition room. "Hi, I'm Sparky Carbin, the audition producer. Come on in and meet all the guys and gals."

Understanding, graceful, the producer puts you at ease and leads you into the control booth. "This is Edwin Booth, one of the writers; V. Charles Farrell, the other writer; Mervin Leroy, the account executive; Booth Farrell, the account supervisor; Leroy V. Edwin, the copy chief; Carla Binner, the production assistant; Farrell Charles, the media supervisor; Binne Carla, producer's assistant; Booth Mervin, the producer; Edwin Mervin, the director; and I'm sure you know Mickey Mouse, the agency talent-casting director on this account."

You smile at each one, trying to remember the names, to sift their positions in order of eminence. You look deep into each person's eyes as you shake hands. You feel, you exude sincerity and attention. Looking a person right in the eye, giving him a firm handshake makes him know that, whatever else, you are ready to do a job of work.

Depending on your persuasion, do not be afraid to express a gentle sexuality at this point. Lick your lips, exude just a pinch of lust that says, "I am yours, do with me what you will." Just a pinch, mind you. Don't give yourself away for a one-line part. You want to avoid desperation. One auditionee licked *their* lips, I am told, and did not even get the part. She does, however, live today in a very expensive apartment on Park Avenue with no name on the door.

Sparky will remain in the studio with you as the closing whoosh of the soundproof door signals the commencement of the audition. It is blast-off time and your nerves are vibrating cords of anticipation. That is your heart resounding with those chimes, but your head tells you that they are the chimes of the cash register, so you manage to cool it.

In front of you looms that control room. The sea of faces behind the glass undulates, searching you for your talent, your proven mediocrity. You feel stripped naked, vulnerable, unable to protect yourself.

The remote-controlled camera, unlike that control room, is mechanical, objective until it suddenly signals you with a little red light.

The loudspeaker above your head crackles to life frighteningly and speaks. "Now, what we want to do is to set the scene for you and you can proceed." One of the waves in the sea of faces is talking. "This is a person who is just coming home from a hard day's work at the world. Alone finally with his bird. The bird is lackluster, droopy. We want to see that little beastie receive the sing-along comfort from you, the signal that the bird will lift our spirits when he gets his seed and make the evening whole again with his song. It's important to you otherwise; if you don't get a rise out of your bird, you get acid indigestion and cranky. Understand? Now you've got to deliver the line to show your bird that good times are a-coming. Understand?"

You nod and proceed to look at the script in this new light. "Kid, one thing." It is another voice. "You're not all that tired, because people don't like to look at tired, sick people on TV. Understand? So don't make yourself too depressed, too tired."

You nod your head and proceed to look at the script in this new light.

"Darling," one of the ladies says, "can you make yourself tired but with a sense of humor? Not irritable and not hilarious. Understand?"

You nod your head and look at the script in this fading light.

"I don't see it as irritable." A voice from the speaker, but it is evidently not talking to you.

"I didn't say exactly irritable or not irritable but with a sense of humor." The retaliation is meant for the other person on the speaker.

Finally, a commanding voice with a comment that is meant for you, "Do it the way we told you, please. O.K.?"

You nod your head.

"Slate the take, will you?" a new voice says. You look at the control room. Sparky taps you on the shoulder and explains that you should give your name and say, "Take one."

"Take one," you say professionally on Take One.

"Thank you. Next person," someone starts to say.

Wait! Assert yourself. They were not even listening. Tell them you haven't read the script yet. Don't let their silence disturb you. It is possible that you may have alienated them with your independence. But remember, they have not even heard you demonstrate your obvious ability to be Everyman or Everywoman. Ask yourself searchingly, if you can, whether or not you feel you have antagonized the group with this forthright display of your integrity. If you feel that they have no right to be angered, if you feel that you are in the right, draw yourself up to your full internal fortitude limit and murmur silently, "Fuck you." If you feel, however, that you have

taken a giant step backward, that your timing has suffered irreparably, that you have already exploded your
opportunity, then say it out loud.

If you are still there, continue the audition.

Gird yourself, draw yourself up to your full impressive
stature and then sag slightly to create the portrait of the
haggard, urban-worn American. Concentrate on the conception for your motivation. Draw from inside yourself,
look up at the control-room window as if that were your
birdie and say, "Now," (pause) "my *bird* is ready whenever *I* am." Do you feel the complete reversal, the tired,
whipped urban dweller, the prisoner, suddenly making
the transformation—stimulating a natural exuberance,
lifting the spirits of animals and humans everywhere
with some inborn courage? Step back from the microphone and catch the plaudits from the control room.

"Kid," the loudspeaker says, "could you play with it a
little more? Enjoy yourself a little."

You speak again into the sensitive piece of iron. This
time, a smile curling your lips as you picture the subject
coming home from the office, having stopped in for a
quick one with a sexually compatible person and also a
drink. The end of a day well spent, joy and good humor
welling up in your vitals, you step through the door of
your home to find your bird waiting for you, waiting
for the treat! You sing out, "*Now, my bird is ready whenever* I am!" You step back to await the reaction. It's what
they wanted. What's better than 100 percent?

The loudspeaker obliges. "Sweetie, a little more sadness and a little less humor." You prime yourself for the
encore. Must be getting close to what they want. But
before you make the delivery, the loudspeaker speaks

again. A different voice. "Hey, baby, try it with a little sadness, but a little humor."

You prepare. What is so hard about becoming a schizophrenic?

The loudspeaker has an afterthought. "Matey, try it with just a touch of chagrin and a tremor of merriment." Wait, someone else is pushing the button in the control room, because the speaker scores again.

"Wait a minute, luv. Mervin had a thought which might make all the difference. Suppose you just throw it away. Say it matter-of-factly, no expression at all."

You await further developments, but none is forthcoming, so you assume that perhaps they really do not know what they want. It's a case of when they hear it they'll know it.

You resume. Casually, you toss your head around. You've seen Bogart do it a thousand times on television. You press your lips together so that the words merely leak out; your mouth is a drippy faucet. "NowmybirdisreadywheneverIam," you mumble.

There is a long silence. You are unable to see the faces in the control room because of the reflection on the glass. You have a feeling that they are discussing you because no one is looking at you or talking to you. You feel isolated, in solitary.

Deep down, however, you are convinced that one of those readings is right. You have been monitoring yourself on your mental TV screen as you spin your recitations. You have done the readings as if the bird could understand. You have motivated yourself for unimpeachable mediocrity, for splendid mediocrity. You feel inspired. You know that no one will be able to follow your act, to soar to greater heights than you. It was right and you know it.

The speaker crackles on. "How do *you* feel about it, baby?" the speaker coaxes. "Is there anything else you want to do with it?"

They hate it. It was all wrong. Do they hate it? Why are they asking for suggestions if they have heard anything faintly resembling what they are seeking? Does it do for the defendant in the dock to suggest a verdict if all the judges in the high tribunal are unable to concur?

If they *were* enamored of a previous version, and you do yet another one, will you turn them off the one they liked and also kill the new one? It is a time for a crucial and final decision.

"Lemme try one more," you say enthusiastically. There is silence. You have said the wrong thing; the secret word is *shit*.

There is no return now. By saying you would like another try, you have implicitly expressed dissatisfaction with whatever is already done.

"Well, go ahead," the voice on the horn says, but the tone says, "Go ahead, loser."

Whatever it is you meant to do is steamrollered by a climactic burst of passionate, genuine hysteria. You have no idea what you are going to do. Somewhere you hear yourself screaming, "Now *my bird is ready ready ready whenever I am!*" Was that you? It was you.

The loudspeaker breaks on immediately and there is, by God, there is applause! There is excitement coming from that little glassed-in courtroom. They liked it!

"What's your availability for the rest of the week?"

someone asks. "We want to shoot it as soon as possible."

Careful, show them that you are in demand. Need they know that there is no activity, no conflict that can stand in the way of this road, this movement to which you were obviously meant to devote your life? "Anytime, anytime you want," you answer.

"How about in two days?" Mr. Starmaking Loud-speaker asks.

"Marvelous. I'm sure I can make it." Well spoken.

But there is a pause before final verification comes through, before they tell you whether to show up at Universal, MGM or 20th Century. Finally the speaker clicks on again. "No . . . no, too soon, pussycat. This is a test campaign and we want to make sure all the elements are correct. You certainly don't mind a test campaign, do you?"

You laugh gaily. "Why should I? If it's good enough for you, it's good enough for me." What difference does it make as long as the long green is on the way? You turn to Sparky, the audition producer, who is sitting in the studio with you. "What's a test campaign?" you ask.

The answer: "Don't worry. They make the commercial and then they take it to a little city that represents a microcosm of the country—Providence, Rhode Island; Leavenworth, Kansas."

"I still get my thousands?" you ask rhetorically, merely for corroboration. You may have tax problems, you reflect.

"Well," comes the cautious advisory, "see, if the commercial scores well in the test, according to the demographics and the reaction of the people, then—"

"The thousands?" you counter.

"Oh, not for the test. For these tests you get a small amount," you are informed.

"I still get my hundreds?" you plead.

"You might get a hundred or so for the test," the producer tells you.

You feel a new surge of power. After all, you have become a bumper guard on the juggernaut of American advertising. "Well—" you laugh—"I could go to your competitors and say to them that I am testing a commercial for Birdseed and *they* might offer me more money and hire me away!" You are laughing, but there is a threat of power waiting to be unleashed. A little stardom goes a long way.

"No," the answer comes, firm and secure, "you cannot work for any competitor until the test is scored in a couple of months, sweetie." You notice that the producer is patting your arm. "Of course, if the test is a flop, you are free to do anything you want."

"A flop!" You are almost surprised to hear yourself shouting. Yet why not shout when the disgusting and degrading thought of a flop had never entered your mind? You, a flop?

What the hell do they know about fancy television in Leavenworth or Providence? A fat chance a person has with those cities. Did one President ever find himself born in either place?

But who knows, maybe television has educated those people. "And if they like the commercial spot in those test cities?" you venture.

"Then, baby, you're in," the producer says, clasping you.

"I get my thousands," you assume, looking at your cuticles like a real winner.

"Unless, of course, they run your commercial as a 'wild spot.'"

"Wild spot?" you whisper, your panic returned.

"Yes, wild spots," the audition producer says. "'Wild spots,' see, are when they put the commercial in just a few cities here and there—but not using a full network."

"Wild spots," you mutter. You are starting to get a sinus attack.

"The trouble with wild spots," continues the pitiless voice, "is that if people see you in New York and Los Angeles, they assume that you're on everywhere in the country. And the advertising people worry about over-exposure."

You stifle a sob. "Wild spots."

"And they say, 'Don't use that actor again. On too many commercials. On TV too much.' So nobody calls you again for a year or so and you aren't making any money."

An inspiration strikes you. "Maybe I shouldn't do this commercial so that nobody gets tired of me. Then if they ever do see me, they'll want to use me because I'm not overexposed!"

"Don't worry," Sparky assures you mechanically, "the test will be a success."

"Well, if the test is a success," you reason, "and they do use the commercial, maybe some other advertising agencies will see me and want to use me for *their* commercials."

"Nah," Sparky naahs, "advertising people don't watch television. They're too sophisticated."

The door to the control-room door springs open and the people beckon you to enter for your triumphant goodbyes. They are vociferous in their praise, lavish in their appreciation of what you have done, evidently pleased that they heard what they hoped to hear.

You are gratified that you have lessened their labors, cut short the grueling process of auditioning anyone else. You shake hands all around, promising to call each one so that the next time you can have a more social relationship.

Sparky escorts you to the exit. Your eyes are moist for each other, telling each other the unspoken things that you knew had been seething under the hard crust of commercialism.

You remember that they forgot to tell you when you will be doing the commercial.

"Can I call you—" you start to ask as you grasp hands for the last time.

The voice is tortured. "Don't . . . don't call me, darling. I'll call you."

You exit. But you know, you know you are crossing a threshold.

Sparky drifts back to the control room and shouts to the engineer at the tape recorders, "Scrap that one! Wipe that tape, Irv, and use it again for the next creep."

CHAPTER SIX

It Ain't an
Art Form

I'll never forget how I explained the generation gap to myself. There always has been a generation gap; it's nothing new. There will always be a generation gap unless yours is the last generation. In which case, goodbye and good luck.

The older generation, even if it is only older by a few years, judges things by the way it has covered its mistakes in the past. Having amassed these booboos, the older bunch evaluates everything on the basis of what has happened already.

The youngsters, with no past and few experiences, have to look ahead because they don't have the repository of mistakes to look back on. They are rarely interested in hearing about the errors made by the other generation.

The newer Americans have decided that Old Lady History is a whore and they want nothing to do with her. They may nibble around her skirts and cop an occasional feel, but they are suspicious that she is so badly soiled that they can only get a social disease by consorting with her.

Because the elders have been disillusioned before, when they hear the neighborhood gossip about the easy virtue of the old girl they become edgy and defensive about History and they show their hostility to youth. Each generation has an advantage over the other. The younger generation chuckles because it knows that the oldsters can never grow young again. The older generation snickers snidely because it knows that the younger generation is going to grow old. There they stand, one generation looking backward and the other looking forward. How can we ever expect them to see eye to eye?

The point is to attempt to find a basis for comprehending what has happened to television and what may be its fate in the next few revolutions. In order to try to second-guess what is going to happen to television and us, we have to behave as if we are the younger generation, believe that we know nothing of the past, that it is all going to start right here—difficult to do if you are over seven years of age, but we have to attempt to forget the *status quo* and everything we have seen. Forget the following.

In our country there never was a game plan for TV; it grew as it grew. But in countries that were less fortunate than the rich United States, they attempted to plan for television by restricting its growth until they could figure out how to handle it. They tried to figure out the upheavals it would effect in the lives of their citizenry: Would it restrict the output of curds and whey; would it keep people from doing what came naturally and restrict population; would it make the people as smart as their leaders and therefore unmanageable; would it make the people want things that the government did not want them to have; would the TV repairman become more important than the ruling junta? These considerations restricted the immediate growth of television in countries around the world, but once they had answered these questions, the countries could proceed to make the same mistakes the United States has made.

In many lands TV and radio are state media, like the sanitation department or the post office. It is difficult for us to imagine state-owned television. Try to think of Bob Hope as a Civil Service employee (with a P 2 rating). Think of Johnny Carson taking the exam at the Federal Building for late-night talk-show MC. Ponder for a moment on Carol Burnett in her mailman's uniform. Think of Christmas. You would have to leave a little something for the garbageman and Walter Cronkite.

In America, even though television is licensed on a stringent basis by the government, the eventuality is that it will become available to the highest bidder. Once a license is issued, it is rarely revoked. There is a form of control through innuendo and pressure, but even with all of the investigations, challenges, contortions and eyebrow raisings, few licenses have been withdrawn. The main determinant for success in American TV is whether you can make money and at the same time manage to keep from antagonizing the community.

Recently an interesting development began to take place. In communities from one end of the country to the other, groups applied to the FCC for TV licenses. It was interesting because the licenses for which the groups were applying belonged to stations in town already on the air. The stations were forced to fight for their lives, and the cases proceeded to wend their ponderous way into the charge, counter-charge and appeal route, which may tie them up until they have found a replacement for television. With the billions of dollars invested in American television stations, speed to divest them of their licenses is not of the essence.

There may be more challenges to the existing set-up, more and more people trying to get into the television-station game, but there are other technical developments that may make such upheavals unnecessary. Stay tuned for a couple of pages and share that mix-up.

Network television did as much to shrink the country as the old railroads. The mayor of Peoria today knows that the mayor of New York has the same urban problems, and the mayor of New York knows that the MTA in his city is as useless as the Transit Authority in Chicago and Boston. It may not help them in the solution of any of their similar problems, but it is nice to know that one's misery is typically American.

In Los Angeles the weirdos may have a different dialect from their counterparts in Houston or St. Paul, but they can tell that their craziness is of a similar unnature, and this gives them the security blanket of identifying with the strange ones in Miami or wherever. Pollution, drugs, poverty, abandoned vehicles are popular from one end of the land to the other, and it all hangs out on the luminous face in the living room. From Maine to California, from the Dakotas to Texas, the entire country is one big used-car lot, and it would not be presumptive to blame television for the ease with which such a situation

developed. The theory of built-in obsolescence in manufacturing found a mouthpiece in television. If everything
we bought lasted as long as it should for the prices we
have to pay, television would have nothing to sell. They
even try to sell you new television sets on television. It
doesn't work out too well because a nice new set looks
terrible when you see it on an old worn-out screen. And
if it looks good, then your present set is O.K. But we are
moving afield of what we are trying to forget.

If the land was united by TV, the nation was also
divided by TV. When you are alone, you can turn inward
your feelings of being downtrodden, paranoid, depressed,
frustrated, discontented and angry. But with TV, think
of the enlightenment, the revelation in tuning in the
other end of the county or the other end of the country
to find people just like yourself who share your emotional heartburn. It gives you strength, it gives you unity,
it even gives you the courage to find out if maybe you
can't organize

And then, when the telly brings into your home the
others, the ones who are responsible for doing the de-
pressing, the frustrating, the angering, the persecuting,
the naughty things that make you feel so put upon, then
you can be compelled to do some terribleness to combat
the oppressors, frustrators, persecutors. Before TV, what
you didn't know was hurting you didn't hurt you so
much.

The well-accoutered, highly paid executives sitting in
their plastic-paneled offices high in televisionland did not
intend to widen the cleavage in the factions in the
country; that would be the last thing they wanted. The
TV hierarchy would have been thrilled and gratified to

find everybody in America in the same frame of mind and
to keep them that way. Why? Not altruism certainly, but
can you imagine trying to sell things—the same things—
to people who can't agree on anything?

Mr. William Waste III, executive vice-president of
one of the largest TV conglomerates in the world, in a
speech entitled "Blessed Are the Bland," which he made
at the annual meeting of the International Radio and
Television Society at the Hotel Casserole in New York,
recently said:

> Make no mistake about it, don't underestimate the
> American people. They deserve America's best and
> we must give it to them. We must make television
> programming appealing to everyone so that they all
> can enjoy it, more rewarding for all of our people
> instead of just a few. It is a mass medium and we must
> give to the masses what will be beloved by most of
> them. And we must work together, hand in hand, for-
> getting our differences to accomplish that goal.

Mr. Waste III was interrupted fourteen times for
bravos! and huzzahs! during a mere forty-five-minute
speech. But his audience was not ecstatic for the seemingly obvious reasons. The truth of the matter is that Mr.
Waste III was speaking in code, and they understood the
full significance of his cryptic remarks.

What his message meant to the assembled contemporaries was more in the following context. Allow me to
translate:

"Make no mistake about it, don't underestimate the
American people." What he was saying was that they
should not underestimate the numbers of American

people, that they were not taking advantage of the full
audience potential available to them; they could get
more viewers.

"They deserve America's best and we must give it to
them." The audience must see the latest American
products, all the good things that America has to demonstrate to them before delivering the products on the in-
stallment plan.

". . . make television programming appealing to everyone . . ." Television programs have to be made blander
so that they don't offend *anyone*. They have to be made
so that no one turns a single show off. They may not turn
it on, but they must not turn it off.

"It is a mass medium . . ." Bring the programs down to
as simple a level as possible.

". . . give to the masses what will be beloved by most of
them." Fill the programs with stories of puppies, children
and mother, and who can argue with that?

The statement ". . . we must work together, hand in
hand, forgetting our differences . . ."—What Mr. Waste
III meant by that was that the networks had better stick
together and all do the same thing. If one network were
to break the block by offering more provocative programs, it would make their expected returns less predictable and therefore more expensive.

He further specified in his famous "Blessed Are the
Bland" speech: "The commercials must carry their own
weight, being just as important as the programs. Their
quality must never be below that of the programs they
enhance."

See that? What he was really saying was that the programs being the carriers of the spots, if the commercials

were great, then they would stand out above the mediocrity of the programs and they would be more forceful
and successful in their sales purpose.

Mr. William Waste III retired from his high network
position shortly after this landmark speech to accept a
high government position. His reward for the work he is
doing in his high government position will probably be
an appointment to private industry, perhaps even to a
high television network position.

In the early days of television in America there were
adventuresome people, inventive shows, but that was
before the days of the demographics and the computers.
If the demographics are the chapter and verse in radio,
they are the entire scriptures of television. Because the
expense of turning out the product is so formidable, the
prospects of making a mistake so dire, financially, for the
producers, those old devil demographics are the life and
death determination in TV. And with computers, in
twenty-four hours it is possible to ascertain whether you
have a hit or whether you had better set fire to your
production facilities for the insurance money.

It may not be true because we are unable really to
check into internal corporation secrets, but they do say
that the third network—no letters mentioned—has a
computer room for the viewing of the statistics after each
show. The room, so we are told, has a window frame, but
no glass, for producers who do not like to cut themselves
as they leap.

It's the cost. The production costs of television shows
are so immense that the old process of manufacturing a
"pilot" show to indicate the nature of a new series has
practically been abandoned. The practice now is to

search and research the demographics of what the public has admired so far to ascertain what they will like in the future. Since demographics cannot tell what they will like if they have never seen a program like the projected one, the figures are less than trustworthy. Besides, the public is not inclined to worry about the television companies and their problems; the public has enough worry simply trying to maintain its own privacy.

All the industry wants to do is to avoid the annual fall bloodletting. It is a financially traumatic experience to see new shows go down the drain. The union fees for the cameramen, the script girls, the lighting people, the prop men, the soundmen, the editors, the film and tape, the directors and producers, the performers make the costs of new shows comparable to the building of a luxury apartment development. Coffee for the crew is $100 a day. Everything is $100, even hello.

The industry, therefore, attempts to use the figures at hand to avoid mistakes, to avert the costly hello and rapid goodbye of a new program. Before the days of the demographics, the numbers, they were forced to rely on *creativity*. Creativity is an eternal problem. Creativity brings new ideas, crosses uncharted frontiers where there are no interstate highways of statistics to guide you. With creativity, you have to have the guts to risk your life, your reputation and, more important than life and reputation, the money, to try a new concept.

The industry has ascertained that statistics are more indicative than creativity. Statistics are the mortal enemy of creativity. With statistics you can only know what has gone before; with creativity you can only guess what lies ahead. With statistics you introduce "discretion." Some crossword-puzzle experts define "creative discretion" as "fear" or "chicken shit."

It might be enlightening to examine how "creative discretion" operates. Let us say that the latest success on TV is a rollicking comedy, ha-ha, humor hour called "Zany-In!" The program was originated by Marvin Producer, in cooperation with David Cooperation and with the assistance of Leonard Assistance. The network has splurged for one half the money it took to get the first hour on the air. The other half of the money came from the associates in cooperation with each other, or from the cooperators in association with each other.

The program got onto the network in the first place because of a rather fortuitous circumstance. Mr. Waste, the head of the network, happened to have been a one-time brother-in-law of Mr. Producer. Mr. Producer had helped the network out of a tight spot and the network was indebted to him. Mr. Producer had, on short notice, provided a one-hour special to replace a network disaster called "College Humor." When Mr. Producer's replacement showed fairly healthy demographics, it was thought that he might come up with another saver. And so he did. He originated, with a little help from his friends and their friends, "Zany-In."

It is a fast-moving hour of madcap goings-on, with just a tinge of pseudo-social significance, a group of attractive young people, an occasional Establishment name—and it hits big in the demographics. Since all of these components have fallen into place, let's see what creative discretion results.

The week following the triumph of "Zany-In," a writer brings a serious script to one of the agents who offers

literary efforts to television. The script concerns the trib-
ulations of a young couple who want to marry but are
faced with seemingly insurmountable problems.

In the script the young hero is a physician whose parents urge him to become a suburban MD. The heroine,
on the other hand, wants him to serve humanity by forging new socio-medical advances among the Eskimos.
There are practically no medical pioneers among the
Eskimos because when you do an examination in an
igloo you can freeze your everything. The story evolves
into the liberation ideals that the young girl brings to
the relationship. The young doctor insists throughout
that she is emasculating him and through the play tries
to keep a firm hold on his masculinity.

In the final scene the young lady runs off into the
frozen wasteland in a symbolic cry for help. There is no
room for laughter in such a tale. It seems, to its author, a
dreadfully important piece of commentary on our times
and on the way things are going to be.

The agent has seen the remarkable accolades that
"Zany-In" received; he is aware of what the new program
has done around the vast nation. Young and old, white
and black, rich and poor have given it the thumbs-up
signal. When the writer steps into the office with his play
for television, "Bossed or Lost," the agent is very re-
ceptive.

"Only one thing," the agent tells the author. "There
are certain fringe changes that you must make so that you
fit in today's genre." The light of recognition burning in
his eyes, the writer agrees that if there is anything he
wants to do, it is to fit into today's genre.

"There will have to be certain structural changes that

we will need," the agent instructs, "certain dramatic pit-
tances which will make the thing move more quickly.
Then I can show it to a most anxious network—they
already know about it—and you will be bathing in offers
for your next piece of work. You must trust me. After
all, don't we both want the same things—the chance to
make a statement and recognition for you as an author
of the first line?"

Why should the writer bother to question such ambitious motives? Why should he fight direction from a
pro? The writer agrees to make the scenes play shorter,
perhaps cut them so that each one runs about three
minutes, ends with a blackout line. He also agrees to
insert several sequences where ice is thrown into the face
of the doctor on the cue line "Shoot it to me!"

The part of the mother of the bride is expanded from
her one-line death scene to several misty appearances
where she is lying on the icy ground shouting, "Here
come de Aurora Borealis!"

The ambitious writer further agrees, although he is
beginning to become a little hesitant, to insert a sequence
where the Vice-President of the United States appears
for a cute appearance pulling a dog sled and saying,
"Mush, mush."

"Trust me," the agent assures the perplexed author.
"I know what they're looking for in the production
centers."

There is one last change: The part of the young man is
expanded to that of a set of twin brothers who are both
mad about the young lady. This additional characterization gives the play a boost, a chance for several playful
interludes of comedy relief that will spark the movement

of the vehicle. The agent assures the writer that such changes do not make a major dramatic difference, but they do allow a certain facility in the handling of sales opportunities when talking to the program purchasers at the networks.

But to the last change that the agent requests, the writer finds himself unable to acquiesce. The agent would like the introduction of some husky dogs as talking characters in the play. "Can you imagine the opportunity for merchandising that these cute little wise-ass dogs will give us? All over the country, kids will be screaming for toy dogs like the ones on the show! We can farm out a hack artist to do a comic strip! The impact of this show will be legend."

Taking a good look at the metamorphosis of his play, the writer protests the dramatic reasoning for some of the changes.

"Let me explain," the agent soothes the disgruntled author. "The essence of television is this: familiarity. As soon as a new program hits the screen, they rate it. If it begins to do well—that is, if it returns the second week —it's a smash. The thing to do, if one desires the boundless returns of television success, is to imitate a successful program as closely as you can. But with a twist!

"O.K., your show will be great because you are imitating one of the biggest successes ever, 'Zany-In,' but with a witheringly clever twist! You are doing the show from the North Pole! That's clever because less inventive people would do their program from the farm and call it 'Awww-Haaaw!' or from New York with young people, or one from downtown Miami. You used your brain, and that's what it's all about. Creativity, but with discretion.

"Now remember, in a medium where imitation is creativity, the use of a talking dog is so far out that they will acclaim the wonder of your genius."

To prove the admiration with which he holds the "Bossed or Lost" script, the agent insists on making the program a weekly show and changing the name of the program, ever so slightly, to "Brrrr-In."

"If that doesn't do it," the agent assures him, "we'll change the story slightly to make the hero a professional hockey player with a black side-kick who acts as his trainer, but they are both, in reality, secret agents. We'll call it 'Ice Pie.'"

"And if that doesn't work?" the writer asks forlornly.

The agent checks his rating standings, what's up and what's down this week. "In that case, we'll make the girl a black teacher who is also a registered nurse specializing in drug addiction among Eskimo college students. And the boy will be a storefront lawyer with a dirty mouth who is always insulting his clients with the clichés of prejudice."

"And if . . ." the author asks.

"Don't worry, kid," the agent reassures him dreamily, "we can always make a singing family out of the Eskimos and call it 'The Rock Family on the Rocks.'"

Remember, we are privy only to what is going on in one agent's office. In talent agencies all over the country they are also attempting to figure out how to produce winners with the least risk to anyone, especially themselves. And most of the other people are not as innovative, as creative as our agent.

Cost. Cost is one of the reasons for the phenomenon of the "talk" shows in television, both here and abroad.

The programs fill time reasonably. Essentially, the talk show is television's disc-jockey show; they are really visual radio shows, the guests filling the time instead of records. Because the same guests spin from show to show, mugging and plugging, the programs are used to fill massive chunks of time with a minimum of production expense. The guests are paid scale talent payments (the lowest union pay), which explains why singers tell jokes, actors discuss politics and comedians explain how sad they are in real life. If they have to act, sing or comede, the price goes way up. Performing is expensive; talk is cheap.

Some of the programs produced in Hollywood and New York are so expensive that they are presented to the public at a weekly loss to their producers. They have to make the money in the reruns of the program, the second, third and hundred and fifth time around. There is an expression which is used for the rotation of reruns and syndicated shows throughout the country: "bicycling."

Movies, reruns, original shows that have never seen network use are bicycled throughout the country, rolling on the screen of one station on Monday and the one in the nearby city on Tuesday. Tapes and films are rolling throughout the nation's TV channels, filling the time, bringing in the viewers and thereby, inevitably, the commercials.

What does the rerun-bicycling mean to the industry and to you, the viewer, sitting there with your tattered demographics hanging out? It means that you are not getting anything new. It means that the bright young comedian who should be breaking in playing Clowny the Clown on the afternoon kiddies' show at 4:30 has no place to start. It means that Rosalie Wingnut, the attractive young girl down the street who has been studying ballet for thirteen years at Mrs. Rose's School of the Danseuse, will never get the chance to entertain the town on the Saturday Night Beer Hall Follies sponsored by Mr. Jules's Jewelry Store. The local dramatic society, which should get a chance to present a few original plays during the year—especially new material written by new local writers—will never get onto the tube if Burns and Allen are available on the cheap.

So what did we end up with? Having reached for the lowest common denominator, having reached for the greatest audience, the industry was faced with a strange juxtaposition. As a standard evening's TV fare there would be a story about a father facing life with his motherless children. Then there would follow a story of a mother facing life with her fatherless children and a ghost. Then there would be, for an encore, fatherless children facing life with a rich uncle and a valet. These were identity situations where the audience was asked to identify with the problems, the everyday little dilemmas, of these families like yours and mine. The main concern of these TV siblings was often how to wangle a new bicycle from Mom, Pop, Uncle or the ghost. For more intricate consideration we had such fare as life with a witch, life with a genie, life with a Martian.

Most of the programs that had any successful continuity were blood relatives to the comic strips in the newspapers. One-dimensional people with talking horses, thinking dogs, the mother was frequently portrayed as a bright, well-intentioned nag. The father was usually characterized as a forlorn, harebrained individual constantly being victimized by his children, his boss and his world. On occasion, for comic relief, the portrayals were reversed so that the mother was harebrained and the father was a nag.

These little gems of escapism were in such conflict with the news programs that followed them or preceded them that it forced TV into the "relevance phase" that we have discussed. Every evening brought its share of a little murder, a little rottenness and a chunk of honest-to-God war right into the same machine which was churning out the troubles of little Herbie and his broken model-jet wing.

"Hey, why don't we throw in a few stories with drugs in them?" asked a bright young executive at Network A.

"Why don't we throw in a few stories about drugs?" asked a bright young executive at Network C.

"Hey, I think I got it," said a bright young man in the mailroom at Network N. "Why don't we throw in a few stories about drugs?" He sent his recommendation to his father, the vice-president, and the young mailroom man was immediately made a group head.

Suddenly all of the networks blossomed with stories about drugs. It seemed as if the same team of writers were running from one network headquarters to the other, passing off the same plot with just a change of faces to protect them from plagiarism.

"We need some good black guys," said Network C. Network A and Network N must have had network ESP, because simultaneously several black police lieutenants, teachers and doctors turned up on the screen.

The routine was repeated with poverty, radicals, pollution and a host of other popular causes which were plaguing the nation. It was nice to know, at last, that when you turned on a little TV for the evening you could catch a couple of hours of uninterrupted anxiety.

Here's the formula. The audience is introduced to a typically Amurican family. It so happens that one of the most lovable members of the clan, usually a person with a weak countenance, brings home a minuscule problem. The entire family is surprised; they had no idea that Mr. Swell Guy was such a sonofabitch. The little problem is really a manifestation of a larger problem such as drug abuse or a twisted libido or maybe an illegitimate child with both problems. Fortunately for the family, they are acquainted with the weekly hero of the series, an outsider who steps in to help because he owes the family something for past favors.

Our hero, the star, is prepared to risk his entire career, his life, his height or something important to help the family out of its predicament. At the end of the episode the star has saved the family member from certain disaster. But before the saving, the member of the family with the problem comes as near to death as possible. He may even die and be brought back to life by the split-second mouth-to-mouth resuscitation of the star of the series.

Before this whole clammy affair is over, the family will be rent asunder, each member having been forced to examine his relationship with the other members, with himself, with the Book of the Month Club and with you the audience. For some reason or other, the star seems to be all-knowing and all-powerful because of a fortunate series of coincidences which recur in different form each week. A feeling. A sense of impending oatmeal—

something—makes that guy make the right move at the proper time. He comes racing across town just at the prevailing moment of greatest tragedy; there is always an automobile chase.

When the situation is solved, everybody lives on, hurt but happier, sadder but wiser, humbled but nobler. One week later the star is back to save another member of another family to whom he owes a favor and . . .

It's all done in a half hour or an hour.

The riddle of reality cannot be deciphered so quickly. (Most of us can't do it in a lifetime.) The problem that was solved by the star of the relevant dramatic show bounces back on the news; an hour later, as full of piss and vinegar as it was before. Since these very same programs will be going into rerun cycles, they may be circulating the stations of the country until solutions are really found for the problems they encompass.

The reality problems were not only useful to move the stories of the prime-time dramas; they were a godsend to the afternoon soap operas. They were relevanting all over the place in the tear-jerkers before dinner hour. With the exception of one vampire story, the soap operas were largely a matter of life and death, and the vampire soap topped them by being a story of death and death.

It is imperative that the dramas, whether they be at night or in the afternoon, be peopled by doctors, lawyers or policemen. With the stories being largely concerned about the exploits of such occupations, you can have at your disposal a constant flow of life-and-death dramas whether they stem from police cases, hospital cases or legal cases. There is always a good case history to make 'em laugh.

After all, what kind of a continuous drama would result if you took for your premise the adventures of "Jeffry Glassman, licensed optometrist"?

Before we forget all that we have seen and heard and learned about television in our time, there is one high-pitched whistle coming from the Federal Communications Commission. The Feds have recognized that network control of local stations' time is not a particularly progressive way of helping the locals to exercise creativity. There is not much opportunity for the development of new ideas if there are only three places to put the new ideas. Three strikes at the networks and you're out. As a result, the commission ordered the networks to relinquish some of the time that they were programming for the local stations.

You may think that the intention of the commission was less commendable than it seems; they may merely have been attempting to loosen the hold that the networks have on such a large number of minds and opinions regarding the government. The FCC, a regulatory body of the Executive branch, may just have been attempting to dilute the political-commentary pipeline flowing from the three networks. After all, if the networks have to cut service to the local stations, they would conceivably eliminate the least profitable services. What are the least profitable things the networks do? News and public-affairs shows. It goes without saying that they are not going to guillotine "Zany-In."

But the station manager of any non-network station (exaltedly called "independents") would be thrilled to inform the network affiliate about the interesting exercise of filling time. The local, independent stations have been confronted for years with the puzzle and it's not like filling time on a local radio station; you can't throw on another three records.

Television stations also differ from radio stations in that they cannot simply adopt a format. There are no television formulas; all the stations are alike. They either have to spend a great deal of money to develop their own programming or they have to buy outside programs from free-lance syndicators and movie distributors. The store-bought commodities are much less expensive for the stations than canning their own lemons.

The people who run the stations work their slide rules into the ground figuring out how to beat the demographics, the syndicators and the other local stations in town. It is strictly mathematics to try to counterattack the other stations. If the networks run a drama at 9:00 P.M., you run a game show. If they run a game show, you run a movie. It's called a counterprogramming, and it would be simple except for one thing: Television movies are limited and there are only so many tried-and-true reruns you can buy to compete with the network shows. And the local programs, excepting news and discussions, are frightfully expensive, and one of the forbidden words in the independent-television vocabulary is that word *Expensive*.

The older generation occasionally speaks in wistful tones of the "golden age of radio." Communications historians—who are specialists in their field like podiatrists are specialists in theirs—tell us that the golden age of radio tarnished in about fifteen years. Television, a much more dynamic medium, has managed to debauch itself in less time than that. It remains with us, fat and sloppy, veils of debilitation covering the vision it once possessed. Its potential unrealized, its plans unexciting, it staggers slowly in place on a treadmill of inferiority.

So far. And that is the take-off point where you must forget everything you know and make an attempt, as the younger generation is forced to do, to forecast what could happen now instead of dwelling on what has been.

The future of television, is it predictable? Did Wilbur and Orville envision the SSTs and air pollution? What further pollution of the air are we speculating about for tomorrow? Listen to what your friendly neighborhood paranoid might say if you could hear some of my most disquieting contrivances.

Right now it is possible to turn on every television set in the country automatically with a single signal from Headquarters that would bring Big Brother (or, for the feminists, Big Mother) or #1 right into your home whether you wanted to see him or not. There he would be at 6:00 A.M., waking you up with the thought for the day and instructions on behavior and conduct for the rest of the morning. The evening hours could be filled with strength-and-joy lectures and exercises on how to turn one's parents in to the secret police. Ridiculous? Unthinkable? Thinkable but not possible? The prospect is not even one for which the engineers must sit and design anything new; it is possible with simple electronic gimmicks we have today, many of which do far more sophisticated jobs than the one I have connived.

Here is the procedure. For about one dollar a small electronic relay—an elementary piece of electrical gimmickry—could be installed in every new television set manufactured after this book is published. Each new set would have the thingamajig in it when it came to the store. You, taking your new television set to your hearth and home, would plug it into the electrical outlet.

#1 in Headquarters could have his communications people send a nationwide pulse through the electrical grid which supplies the nation's power, and your set would pop on whether you wanted it to or not. And there he would be, #1 with his message for the morning. Of course, #1 would still be asleep; it would be a videotape.

I have set the price at one dollar because I wanted to allow for inflation. The actual cost would be less when the installation is done on a nationwide, wholesale basis. You might contend that the legalities necessary for such an eventuality would be outside the realm of feasibility in our country. I wish I could agree with you, but under the guise of an emergency broadcast warning system to improve our current one, which was erected to protect us in national emergency, the law could be belted through in a routine fashion. Unfortunately, our current emergency broadcast system has demonstrated several times that it could stand improvement.

Only, what is an emergency? What is considered an emergency today may not be considered an emergency tomorrow, and what is unthinkable today may be considered tomorrow a thinkable enough emergency to cause the installation of the little turn-on gismo.

Realistically, it probably never could be done. It would cost too much more as soon as it became a government project. It would probably cost us $1.25.

There are more heartening ways of getting everybody into the act. In the laboratories of the world they are spending millions of dollars—they already have invested

millions of other dollars—to bring those errant eyeballs
back to the tube. The way is being cleared to exploit
containerized programs, cassettes, video discs and 3-D
systems. What will eventually join the record player and
audio tape player in your home entertainment system
is a video record player of one kind or another.

The plan seems to be that when you come home from
a hard day, wherever you spend your hard day, you will
throw a disc or a cartridge into the old player and sit back
and enjoy the video presentation of your varied choice.
What do you say we see *Citizen Kane* tonight? How
about a delightful program of Beethoven with the London Philharmonic? Maybe you would rather rock a little
with the Gribonis, the new group which has just been
acclaimed as the finest singing ensemble since the Beatles.
Or maybe more to your taste is a presentation of a lecture
on the molting habits of the South American chuwanda.

You might have the discomfort of having to take out
such treasures from your local lending library or you may
be able to purchase them outright. Who knows whether
these cassettes might not even turn up at the local druggist's or the discount feed store next to the pizza joint?

The systems are available already; several are on the
market. But an industry which remembers two fiascos is
not so pleased to make it a trio. The struggle for com-
patibility is being waged now, in advance, to prevent re-
currences of the two financially destructive encounters
over the RCA-CBS color television systems and the
RCA-Columbia Record LP vs. 45 rpm records. At this
moment there are at least six systems under consideration
and on which one is the winner rides a mighty sum of
potential money. It is possible that there will be more

than one winner in the race to covet containerized programming.

Engineers have reported the plausibility of the development of 3-D television through the utilization of laser
beams and holograph systems. At this moment, the control of the lasers is still too unpredictable to use with live
actors. But some day—some day—you may well be sitting
in your living room or wherever you may sit for tomorrow's viewing and have your very favorite beloved star,
dead or alive, virtually walk into the room. You may be
able to run up to the figure and say what you have always
longed to say, "Why are your shows so bad?" The technical people have already shown their creativity; it is now
up to the creative people to show theirs.

What is going to be on the video cassettes, the video
recordings, the cartridges? Will appearances in containerized shows preclude appearances on live television?
Will we get another rehash of the old shows and the old
movies—things that television has rejected or discarded?
The speculation has promised days of golden viewing,
but that is why they call it speculation.

There have been predictions that in the next few years,
give or take a million dollars, every available production
facility in America will be whirring with activity. Producers will spray into your grasp everything from the
annals of civilization to cartoons on some kind of cassettes
which plug into the player of your set or onto discs whose
grooves can be translated into sight and sound at your
command. According to the fanciful view of the pre-
dictors, no longer will you be forced to tune through
five or six channels of pap to select the least degrading
way to spend an evening. With the availability of laughs,

lives, loves, art, how-tos, how-not-tos and whatever-be-came-ofs, you will be the master of your viewing leisure for a small rental cost or a slightly increased personal library cost. The equipment is almost there. The programs must certainly come, and it is to be hoped that this is a harbinger of better viewing.

It is conceivable that you will be able to procure an entire college education not through the varied treasuries of Harvard, MIT, Stanford and schools which have the capabilities of the vast uplifting of the entire nation; your belly telly may be the seminar of the future. There may be a means to learn languages by stopping the disc or the cartridge to answer such world-shaking questions as *"Où est le crayon?"* Medical practitioners in faraway places may well be notified of advances in technique by the Operation of the Month Club; dentists may be filled in too. Mechanics may learn their entire theory by the simple expedient of inserting a cassette into a player, if they can figure out how to make it work. Business may conduct office seminars and keep abreast of what is going on in the home office by frequent tapes from the president.

For the more esoteric tastes there may well be the most varied selections of explicit erotica ever imagined by the fertile mind of mankind. Without even trying, I have already dreamed up the first in an endless series of probable recorded television shows that will live in infamy, and I am sure that you have your own suggestions for suggestive variations in viewing.

It is evident why the Supreme Court has trod so lightly in cases where it has been requested to rule on the definition of obscenity. The guidelines they have been struggling over are hardly for today; the rulings for obscenity are for tomorrow, when the landmark decisions will govern the kinds of funny things we may want to show in our homes to our friends and neighbors. When the product is brought into the home, innocent eyes protected from its observance, who is to be the arbiter of what you can or cannot see? If I happen to have prurient eyes (from the song of the same name), can the Supreme Court or Sergeant Friday come bursting in and tell me what I can or cannot do with my home TV screen? Can you tell me what will turn me on or can I turn off what turns you on?

As another involvement, some of the equipment involved in the revolution in videoland offers the use of your own movie camera, if your own movie camera uses Super 8mm film, and some of the equipment utilizes inexpensive videotape camera set-ups. With the videotape cameras you have the movie version of picture-in-a-minute versatility that Dr. Land's Polaroid brought to still photography. Hear the clarion call of your best friends as they ask you to rush over to view the latest trip to Grandmother's that they made with the kids and the dog. See what your neighbors did, constructed a four-hour television show using no talent but their summer vacation. If home movies made enemies out of lifelong friends, think of what television home tapes will be able to do; the lights will remain on, and sleeping through the show will be impossible.

Happily, there will always be friends who have the kind of movies that real friends have; then there may be some value to the call to come and see the latest of the adventures of the masked partners. Where do they get those movies anyhow?

And with your own camera, you may have a whole tomorrow of remembering yourself in vivid, living color on your home screen in pictures that you wouldn't show to your best friends. With pictures like those, you may never turn back to the news.

How far away is this wonderland of viewing delights? Jack Gould, the TV oracle of the New York *Times,* feels it is farther away from our eager grasp than we would like to contemplate. On November 15, 1970, his summation in the twenty-pound Sunday edition of the paper was entitled "The Great Day Isn't Exactly at Hand," and he cautioned the public to refrain from premature investment in imperfect hardware, an admonition which means it is closer than we think.

The technical publications—you know, the ones with all those funny lines and πR^2s in them—have been detailing the equipment, spelling out the similarities and differences in the various discs and cartridges for several years. Since about 1969 the newsstand publications, such as *Popular Photography* and *Modern Photography* and *Jack and Jill (Jack and Jill* has not mentioned it, but I still buy it), have been discussing the prospects of the video cassettes and the discs and their effects on amateur photography. After all, uses of the camera such as the ones envisioned are in their bailiwick and they are showing proper interest.

The unions representing people employed in television, American Federation of Television and Radio

Artists (AFTRA) and Screen Actors Guild (SAG), have been holding conclaves—sometimes even together— concerning the future of their actors and actresses in the home video picture picture. The two unions have little to distinguish their functions. AFTRA represents performers who work live and on *tape;* SAG represents performers who work on *film.* It is a somewhat incestuous relationship since often it is the same performers who must join both. With the picture as clouded for these performers as it is in the future mixture of tape and film, films-on-tape and tapes-on-film, some people think that these two old circling tigers should agree that in a union of unions there is strength.

SAG well remembers the struggle they had when television began its use of films that had been made prior to TV. The fight to get residuals for performers and their old films was less successful than if everyone had antici- pated the national late show. Apparently AFTRA and SAG figure they are not going to be taken down the primrose path again, and their current concern indicates that the chorus line of video cassettes, *et al.,* is getting ready to stick its chewing gum behind the curtain and dance onto the stage.

ASCAP, the American Society of Composers, Authors and Publishers, and BMI, Broadcast Music Incorpo- rated, the guilds protecting songwriters, are scurrying to carve out codes to guard their members from the un- authorized use of their creations. They point with trembling hands at the years of pirating of music that have resulted from inadequate protection from devices such as the jukeboxes—pirating that still goes on today.

The performers and the other creative people evidently believe that if video fantasyland is tomorrowland, it's only a rainbow away. (Copyright 1972.)

With such equipment as the little fulfillment generator atop your TV set, with your own programming, there will no longer be the need to write the FCC to harass a sponsor or question the taste of the broadcasters. Anybody, everybody can be his own program director or his own censor. You will be the one to decide how the little electronic pump will inundate you.

Unless . . . unless, of course, you have cable TV. Then you have another revolution that could erupt. You thought you were at the end of the phosphorescent delights glimmering across your face. There is still cable TV. So far, cable TV does not grow everywhere; its natural habitat is any area where ordinary run-of-the-mill television cannot be received very well. If you live in an area already served by cable TV, allow me the indulgence of explaining what it offers to those who have never seen it.

The idea of cable TV was to bring the miracle of the age into places where natural or man-made obstructions made ordinary reception impossible, to places where distances from TV stations made reception so trying that people were popping aspirins like gum drops, to isolated communities too small to support their own TV stations. The cable was brought into the home or the apartment like a telephone wire and the TV set was connected to the wire.

Let's take an imaginary city—call it Atlantic City— Atlantic City; obviously there could be no place by that name. Our imaginary city is just outside the reach of TV signals from places such as Philadelphia, New York and Baltimore—which to our imaginary residents is a blessing. After all, they have the wind and the sea and their cavities full of salt-water taffee. A fellow resident sets up an expensive antenna on an imaginary sand dune somewhere and puts together powerful amplifiers and boosters and he is able to receive programs from places like New York, Philadelphia and Baltimore. He might even connect a cable to the antennas of other fellows, farther away in the state, who have similar antennas but who can receive the signals from different cities.

Then our man says to the imaginary residents, "Hey, everybody, for two cents a month" (I told you it was imaginary) "I will run a wire into your house and you can get television on every channel on your television set."

The residents might say, "O.K., stick the wire into the house," and they're all in business.

Now our cable operator says, "Folks, you notice we don't have our own television station in Atlantic City. How about on one of the channels I throw in a little movie now and then and your local merchants can sell your taffee and parasols directly to your neighbors and the pigeons staying at the local hotels?" O.K., say the local merchants because they have been looking for a way to beat down the advertising rates in the newspapers anyway.

One night, after a visit to another imaginary city, our cable person realizes that if he were to knock another out-of-town channel off, he could take an X-rated movie, a basketball game or a Broadway play and put it into the cable. He could jam it with electronic sounds and scramble the picture. But if the home folks added fifty cents to their monthly payment, he could remove the jamming and the scrambling. *Voilà,* pay TV!

Throughout the country, in mountainous areas which defeated the airborne signals and smashed them into the ground, in cities where the metallic skeletons of buildings chewed up the transmitted signals, little men with big eyes were duplicating in reality the shenanigans of our imaginary operator from imaginary Atlantic City. Some of the operators even went so far with their inventiveness as to chop out the commercials that were coming along with the programs and replacing them with their own. Wasn't that cute?

The local stations and even the television networks suddenly realized that there were a few questions that should be pressed. Who owns the programs? Can they be fed into a cable and wired into homes with no payment to the producers, writers and performers who bore the program? Can a cable company throw out a commercial and insert another without some sort of contribution to the originator of the program? To put their wonderings another way, "How can we make a buck out of this?"

The government began to rattle its bureaucratic brains and ask a few beauties of its own. Is a cable company that uses wires but does not operate out of state regulable? Are copyright laws applicable to these companies which lift the programs and pump them by wire without paying any creative kopecks at all? Is a cable company like a telephone company that operates locally? If one cable company connects to another in a different state, isn't that a federal concern? To rephrase their speculations, "How can we make a buck out of this?"

The FCC decided to set a limit on the operations of the cable carriers. With an "Aw shucks, fellas" attitude, they established jurisdictional guidelines for the cablers. What the Commission attempted was to prevent the cable operators from injuring established local TV stations by limiting the kind of services the cables might pro vide in the major cities. The FCC also insisted that each cable operator must keep available at least one channel for the exclusive use of civic and public interest groups, a channel, incidentally, on which the operator may not make a profit.

The operators have agreed to these restrictions almost joyfully so eager are they to get their businesses rolling. They know that today's FCC will not be tomorrow's FCC and tomorrow may bring concessions, turnabouts and pleasant little surprises that will make the whole business worthwhile. For as the Pharaohs of old used to say, "When you're building something, it's best to get in on the ground floor."

Wait a minute, what's that up in the sky? Is it a bird, is it a plane, is it Superman? No, it's a satellite! What's that chunk of space junk got to do with the price of television eggs? The commercial satellite people, a private company in which some of you may hold shares, and the American Telephone Company, a private company in which some of you may hold shares, have those space marbles floating around out there for more than just progress reports.

They are calling, "Why not bounce signals from TV stations off the satellites and have the home sets fixed so that they can receive them? If the home sets can receive pictures from the satellites, let's avoid the middleman, the networks, and not wire up anything—no cables, no cross-country network lines. Why, a station can beam out a program from Los Angeles and have it picked up by ordinary everyday people in New York or Bridgeport! We could have the marching band from Reno, Nevada, entertaining the annual lobster fest in Bangor, Maine, and you wouldn't even need a foot of wire." Electronically it's feasible and the possibilities are yours to imagine.

Between the cassettes, the discs, the cartridges, the cables, the satellites and the established television stations and networks, the war is about to be waged. It can only be good for the consumers because they will have a list of options undreamed. You may be able to turn a switch, push a button, click in a cartridge to have your choice of a hundred different audiovisual activities a night. It's only a few technical glitches and a hundred legal technicalities away.

But there is another joyful cackling going on simultaneously. It is the sounds of anticipation of the producers, the writers, the actors, the creative people who are eagerly awaiting the first creative breakthrough since the advent of early television. There's no point in inserting a cassette, in turning a switch, in pushing a button if all that emanate from the screen and loudspeaker are a glare and a buzz. There will have to be a gush of ideas and an army of personnel to put it all down on the plastic. There are only the stumbling blocks of time and money waiting to be cleared away before the joyful sights and sounds start bursting from the moribund television set.

Wait, there's another, dissonant, unenthusiastic sound. It is the combined wailing of the movie exhibitors, the theater owners and the literary world. What happens to the movie house, the legitimate theater, the magazines and books which are rolling out every day when the populace has the facility to view and hear all of the viewings and hearings there will be?

Will the self-conducted programming that all the cassette pushers and the dial twisters accrue in the next few years empty out the theaters, the movie houses the libraries? If the exhibitors panic as they always do, yes. If the legitimate theater, the off-Broadway theaters pander to the quick buck, it must happen.

But with all of the home-appliance entertainment facilities, will the wife find remaining at home any more enticing that she has found it after spending a full day there? Will the youthful seekers of fun and gladness be content to remain in their apartments night after night feasting their eyes and ears on the augmented offerings of the funny box? How many people go to the drive-in movies exclusively for the movie?

Evidently the most summoning of the road-show attractions will still be cabled into public theaters for paid attendance. No doubt the best movies and shows will still be a long time coming into the home receptacle. Unquestionably, the attraction of a live ball game will still draw millions to the flu and arthritis of the football stadia throughout the fall.

Or perhaps all of those old habits are among the things that we shall have to forget as members of the older generation. Maybe we have to look forward to the changed environment where the pollution keeps everybody indoors or underground. Through viewing, the eyes will grow immense and the ears will become parabolic reflectors. What a generation gap those people will provide when they are so entertained they are unrecognizable!

CHAPTER SEVEN

So It Ain't a Game

The following is brought to you without the cooperation of the cómmissioner of the league. Any unautho-
rized use of this material as entertainment will be subject
to prosecution to the full extent of credibility.

Ladies and genetlemen, our National Anthem.

And now the game.

In the ancient days of our world, war was the number-
one entertainment in which people could participate.
Outdoors. Indoors, they had each other.

With the advent of the TV era, the locales reversed.
It became possible to enjoy war on the TV indoors, while
sex was frequently moved outdoors. Or anywhere.

Mankind also invented an imitation of war called
sports. It had many of the same strategic elements, but it
was safer and therefore apparently not as much fun. Before television, conflict, real and simulated, was visible
to but a few blood-lovers at a time, the remainder of the
fans being able to follow it only in the press and radio.

For a time it seemed that television was going to make possible the enjoyment of warfare in your very own home. They began to refer to incursions, protective reactions and waste rather than saying invasions, sneak attacks and killings. It enhanced the play-by-play as they covered the moves and improved the game-plan discussion as table talk. And they posted the casualty scores daily.

But warfare proved uncontrollable for television, too haphazard and expensive to follow. So television began to fill time with sports fare.

It was certainly more manageable. It didn't take more than thirty seconds before the commercial interests realized that they had at their dispersal disposal the elemental representation of the human struggle. And with TV, the promoters could control the struggles, time them so that commercials could be injected and even contrive which sporting wars would be seen and which could be withheld from viewing.

When television gave everybody a fifty-yard line, ringside seat for the miniature wars sports represented, it even knocked real war out of the running for top audience interest. You could regulate the sporting wars for first-class production, a little instant replay, and it kept the bookmakers home at night working.

The most combative, the most competitive sports became parlor games. The kill or be killed of athletic games was brought into the homes of people who had never known the difference between a Louisville Slugger bat and the spikes on a pair of tasseled golf shoes. Grandmothers could sit at home and join the maniacal fervor of the local hockey team or enjoy the killer instinct of the hot red-dog squad of their football favorites. People who never cared about the difference between an earned-run average and a birdie or a bogie could still enjoy the participants of a host of sports at their own leisure and their own pace.

The all-seeing cameras allowed the viewers to know the playing fields as only the players had known them until that time. Now, *you* the viewer were in the plays, *you* the viewer were scratching on the pitcher's mound and in the batter's box, *you* narrowly averted a hernia facing off. Everybody became an armchair quarterback.

Television paid for these games, colossal amounts of money to make the owners comfortable and to buy new uniforms for the players. And television resold these games to sponsors who were willing to spend more money to have you see their messages between the plays, the innings, the rounds, the periods.

Because they have been hailed as such a marvelous escape valve for the hostilities of the public and because there is such a strong vicarious feeling about the athletic wars, sports enjoy a peculiar position of immunity in the public mind. Otherwise, some people might call them a monopoly or something dirty.

The courts have decided on several occasions that there's no other business like sports business. The President, when he can find a team in Washington, throws in the first baseball. Until recently, Congress had given games preferential treatment. Now there are some rumblings of critical dyspepsia from Congress, but after a few publicized investigations and a few season passes, the antacid of time will quiet the burblings.

Sports have taken on the mantle of a public service,

like a public utility. You will notice, however, that there is no Public Service Commission for this utility. The owners of the teams, after all, possess a piece of property that they claim represents the community. The teams fly the colors of the city they stand for; the Dallas Cowboys stand for Dallas, the Chicago Bears are a little piece of Chi, etc., etc. The promoters are involved in public relations for the city that their team represents. Every time you say the Orioles, you are saying Baltimore. When you love or hate the Athletics, you are talking Oakland. Hip, hip hooray for the old home team!

The owner of the club, that public-spirited citizen, is in reality a king, an emperor. His domain, the old home team, is a country of its own. When he decides that home is not giving him sufficient return for the team, he attends a summit conference with the other sultans of the other home teams. He informs his fellow rulers that he ain't cutting it in his home, that he wants to move the team. Permission is granted with the proviso that he protect the territories of the other untouchable potentates.

Stop cheering; your home team just left home.

In spite of this lack of loyalty on the part of the team, the fans, for some reason, usually take the side of the team against a recalcitrant athlete. They will be highly indignant toward the star athlete who balks at signing his contract when he is in his prime. When he holds out for what the team screams is an impossible deal, the cries of "What does he want for chrissakes for playing the game?" and "Who the hell does he think he is?" ring through the land.

Who is he, that star? He is General Eisenhower, the Red Baron, Gary Cooper and Peter Pan all rolled into one package of drawing card which has a very limited time to capitalize on itself. And if he should be injured, if he should irretrievably rip some remote part of his anatomy in a three-second grandstand play, he hastily enters the book of historical statistics. He goes from six figures to a very lonely figure immediately. He has no control over his future and no way to bargain except to refuse to play until he receives a figure that can live in the neighborhood that he thinks he is worth.

The clubowners weep that they have a tremendous problem. They can only afford a certain amount of money for salaries. There has to be an end, doesn't there—or the team becomes a losing proposition. In addition, the star interferes with their rights to run the kingdom in the manner in which the owner sees fit. There must be some merit to the argument.

However, the team can trade the trouble-making athlete; it is difficult to imagine the athlete trading the Dodgers, and he is not allowed simply to move on to the highest bidder. The athlete is on the gum cards for a very few competing years; the team can grab new rookies each season. There are no rookie competitive ball clubs moving into town each year to threaten the home team. So if the athlete becomes too provocative to the owner, the owner can bring the athlete crashing down to earth anytime he wants. Because, fans, it's the owner's game and he has the ball player by the ball.

Paradoxically, this aggravation to the king of the home team has resulted from the good offices of his benefactor —television. When the close-up lenses of the TV camera began to acquaint everyone with the facial contortions, the moods, the attitudes of the athletes, the fans became more familiar with more of the big-timers. You didn't have to be a star to be a star.

The owners realized that television had done away with the phantom athlete. Building attendance at the parks and augmenting the ratings for the televised games, the owner was forced to promote and feature his players in the same manner that show business builds its money-makers.

And who can blame the stars for beginning to believe their own publicity? The owner had built himself glam-orous monsters, essential and profitable but a terrible pain in the neck of the autocratic owner at the same time. It's a dilemma the sports promoters share with show promoters like David Merrick and Otto Preminger.

Now that TV had these great game shows, it exerted mountainous pressure for a blossoming output on the tube. The sponsorship and ratings ascended with a veloc-ity that would bring tears to the myopic eyes of any comptroller. There are people who speculate that the reorganization of the football and baseball leagues and the basketball merger possibilities have been generated not by the population explosion, affluence of the country, love of the games but the need for a more salable product to fill the stage.

The reorganizations and mergers can provide new playoffs, and playoffs of playoffs, games to fill dozens of hours of previously barren airtime. And with the new material available in exhibition (pre-season) games, the sports fan can feast his eyeballs on seven plethoras of competition. The basketball pre- and post-season opera-tions so far seem to be the winner, giving the fan a season that lasts almost eight months of viewing. There is al-

ways something going on in sportsland TV these days,
a constant road company playing somewhere for television to answer the insatiable demands for shows.

All this activity opens the floodgates of theory as to
what is happening. What is all this sports activity on
television doing to the games? You have come to the
right person.

Look what happened to wrestling. How many Americans can remember the old days of wrestling before television when a couple of salamis would come into the
squared circle and ad-lib a few throws and holds until
one of them couldn't raise his back off the mat by even a
couple of fingers? An honest attempt by two guys to kill
each other, something you could depend on. Then tele
vision began to package the salami and wrestling became
a tame version of "All in the Family."

How do we know that this is not going on in other
sports in answer to television's demand for more and
more show biz? Is there any one of you who can swear on
the life of his picture tube that your favorite sport is not
being manipulated, paced, edited for television?

Look at the evidence I have gathered that will posi-
tively assure you that there is good reason to suspect that
soon all sports on television will be as phony as wrestling.
If you find these revelations offensive, consider how I feel
telling you things that your leading sports writers and
sports commentators have been hiding from you for years.

Look at the players today. Do they look like athletes?
Where are those great old faces of the pugs and jocks
of yesteryear? It must be obvious to even the most avid
sports fan that today's television sports performers are
selected for their over-all good looks, acting ability and
fitness for the role of "star."

When scouts roam the hinterlands these days, combing the colleges for grist for the pro mill, they're not looking for athletes; they're looking for men who *look* like athletes. If one of the scout's selections should happen to have the capability and mentality to be a great player, the scout won't turn him down, of course, but neatness and originality count for more.

If you insist on facts to back up these allegations, here they are. In a secret survey immediately hushed up by the commissioner of the leagues, of the number of rookies entering professional televised sports, over 80 percent said that sports was their second choice for a career. Of that 80 percent, their preferred occupations included movie actor, tap dancer, urologist, leather-belt whittler, flower arranger, glass blower, pizza roller, plastic molder, music teacher and one procurer, whatever that is.

The unquestionable motives for the acceptance by these men of lucrative contracts were as follows: lucrative contracts, access to television cameras and free stuff from sponsors.

The 10 percent who did admit to having a first-choice occupational preference listed their second-choice occupation as sadists and masochists. The remaining 10 percent who entered professional sports gave such varied motivations as "I wanted to make my mother happy," "I like to be near naked men" and "I didn't want to leave the country or register as a C.O."

Don't tell me you haven't noticed the new uniforms. They are a dead giveaway that the games on TV are virtually Broadway productions. When you sit in the stadium, the newer baseball and football uniforms appear identical to the older, less mod ones. On camera, however, it is quite obvious that the fine hand of the costume designer has been hard at work. The new uniforms are tight, oh so form-fitting and as revealing as were the chorus girls' costumes of but a few memorable years back.

It has been attested by one network official who refuses to be quoted that the shots of the new football uniforms in the huddles accounted for several previously untapped rating points in women and folks of homosexual inclination. The testimony is doubtless true because of two developments which lend it credence. Prior to television coverage, there were few *defensive* huddles; now the camera closes in on offensive and defensive huddles continually. Secondly, the penalties for delay of the game—taking too long in the huddle merely to satisfy the cameras—these penalties have dramatically increased.

Baseball uniforms have come under scrutiny more recently, and the costume designers have rendered the svelte lines of the athletes as visible as decency will permit. Basketball players give no quarter to the liberated woman when it comes to the hot pants worn on the courts these days.

The costuming of all the teams has been checked through the computers to see which colors give heightened viewing pleasure and which colors leave the audience uninterested. As a footnote, in Paris in 1972, one of the most *au courant* fashions was the wearing of counterfeit players' jerseys by both young men and women who had no conception of the origin of their colorful outfits. They knew only that it was the latest.

In the area of actual play, there have been developments of which you are sure to be incredulous. We ask only that you are informed of these gestures toward art in the games and believe what your indoctrination will allow you to accept. A leading scout for one of the expansion teams has insisted that all plays are run in football with an eye to their dramatic quality more than their effect on the game score. Under this heading come such devices as (a) passes in situations where runs might have been more productive, (b) incessant use of wide receivers who run across the line, up and down the field to give the impression of intense action, (c) the phenomenally increased number of critical fumbles for surprise.

The permission to return field-goal attempts was a newly won concession from the league because it increases movement on the field by 13.2 percent in games played on natural turf, 11.2 percent on astro turf. Plays that are solid ground gainers but which lack the carefree abandon that the crowd loves are usually phased out by secret order of the commissioner of football if the networks complain. He would probably deny this, but then who could blame him?

If all these revelations seem impossible to you, would it seem unbelievable to you that more and more professional football teams have been sneaking in choreographers to the training camps in the first two weeks? They arrive as professed defensive backfield coaches, but what coach wears ballet slippers?

Not one coach in any conference will admit that he has been taking instruction in choreography—i.e., how the artistic flow of human activity on the field should look. Yet each one of the coaches forces himself to spend hours every week viewing movies of the preceding games. What are they really looking at?

Baseball is not exempt from the show-biz revolution

brought on by TV. In addition to the costuming revisions there is the open admission that the game has been speeded up. There has been a clandestine order to hold down the number of "perfect games" because until the latter innings of such a game a perfect game is a perfectly dull game. As if to reinforce this secret protocol, the ball itself has been progressively hopped up so that hits are possible where only paltry pop flys would have existed pre-television.

Now listen to this. Not one reporter has ever attempted to measure the distances from home plate that are marked off on the outfield fences of the new stadiums. What this freshly disclosed secret means is that the new edifices are being built with greater home-run potentialities to hypo the interest in the game. Is 400 feet as marked on the fences really 400 feet? Or would a Babe Ruth, hitting today, end up with 120 home runs? No one has an available answer.

The seven-foot basketball player is a product of the television age. Check back in the record books and you will discover that high scores such as those that flash on your TV screen today would have been fantasy in the days when the game was more important than the show. Tall men are needed to get those baskets, to keep those points and ratings rolling.

Can you stand to hear about hockey? Hockey fights have always been part of the game, but television has made them mandatory. Low scores are prevalent in hockey not because it is so difficult to get the puck in the cage but because the athletes are hired for their pugilistic ability, not their aim. A hockey game on television without a battle royal would be "Ice Capades."

A more painful revelation is yet to come. When you read it here for the first time you will be able to explain oddities in the sports world which may have baffled you for several years. Seemingly incredible for the old-timers, it is a most natural outgrowth of television coverage of athletic events and it happened without malice and intentional deceit.

Perhaps you have had occasion to ponder the rising rate of questionable decisions being made by officials at sporting events for the past five years. The answer is that more bad decisions have not been handed down; television has made the entire aspect of the game more available. The TV viewer has a less encumbered view of the various games than does the official these days. Long lenses, close-ups, instant replays, all of the electronic ocular aids have rendered the judges, the referees, the umpires the victims of a great degree of obsolescence. Everybody else can see the plays with greater accuracy than the officials. In case of dispute, the incident can be instantaneously repeated and repeated until the quarrel is settled.

What to do with the officials whose uniforms are almost as familiar a part of the game as those of the players? There is an obvious answer. The officials have a new function: to help produce the games for the television commercials. It was a natural genetic development.

Time outs on the football field are determined by the television umpire. It is his obligation to inform each team of its turn to take time out for a commercial. It is also his decision, this television commercial umpire, to appoint certain players who must appear to be winded or slightly injured. He also designates which team must suffer time-consuming penalties when an extra spot is required. Calling in the yard markers and the two-minute warning are also in his province of responsibility. Since the system was installed in 1969, no game has suffered the loss of a single commercial thanks to the efficiency of these dedicated officials.

The baseball umps are as resolute in their pursuit of the commercial schedules as are their brethren in football and basketball. When the commercials are running behind or when the game sinks below its anticipated excitement rating, delays, rhubarbs and ejections are summoned up. Who better than an umpire can determine these happenings since, today, he has so little else to do?

Does this mean a diminution in the "honesty" of the game? Let's not consider honesty in the context that the normal world considers honesty; rather it is the honesty of an entertainment performed to the best of the ability of all the participants that we must consider the question. Having considered the question, let us move on.

There have been changes in the presentation of national sporting events of which the public heartily approved. These show-business-oriented changes have been accepted by the public with nary a whisper of dismay, without a splinter of disdain. For good reason, they are insignificant in the flow of action; they are just tradition. The half-time festivities.

Half-time festivities have been part of the games since the early twentieth century, but what are they? They are stretch time, ablution time, refill-the-old-tank time. Consequently, it was decided by the television networks and the football conferences to standardize the half-time activities to make them the same for all games. Since 1969 all half-time activity shown on television is the same film clip, always the same. It is a segment of film made for a television movie which was never shown because it offended the National League officials in its portrayal of the commissioner.

The home audience is well aware that it is the same film clip in every game, but they accept it for what it is in the same manner in which they accept the laugh track on situation comedy.

Have you ever wondered why they installed synthetic turf in the stadiums? Show-biz tradition. Tradition demands a certain look about a sporting event, and show biz enforces the demands. The blue sky, the green, green grass, the colorful uniforms of the two dreadnaughts rolling toward each other past the hillsides of cheering healthy faces—that was the setting. It all began with the Houston Astrodome, which is the most spectacular television theater in the world: controlled atmosphere, controlled lighting, controlled colors, controlled telecasts.

Other cities, jealous of the culmination of show-business conditions owned by Houston, installed their own version of perfect turf, hoping that their TV setting would come up with classic grass to set off their new uniforms and the collage of their spectators.

That they came up with a significant increase in bumps, burns and breaks was only incidental to the improved quality of the picture. They play must go on, even if it is going on on a slippery hunk of carpeting that could give you such a blister!

Are you beginning to feel doubt? Do you consider these disclosures an exaggeration or perhaps a mammoth insult to your sporting proclivities? Did I lie to you?

I lied to you. I told you that the athlete who was finished in sports was finished.

When the camera turns to the press box during a game, or in between periods, or during a lull, who is there, six feet five and 250 pounds of brawn outfitted in styled hair and latest designer attire? Mr. Athlete. The perfect picturization of the sports player, no longer confined to the field, now pitching the razor blades, end-running around the latest car models, dribbling the cereal commercials.

Fading into the background, trying to be seen behind the nine-foot shoulders of the retired pro, is the old-time sportscaster, slipping into the limbo of kinescopes, black-and-white picture tubes and Jackie Gleason shows. The old-breed sports caller is being phased out in favor of the image of the star, the way television feels that you want your sportscasters to look.

The new breed? They acquit themselves admirably because they've been training while they have been playing, learning to speak, learning to do commercials, to be interesting in their personal lives so that the fans can follow their exploits. To put it more succinctly, players have been performers for some time.

They have not been performers long enough to realize that they are being exploited in a manner that the other television performers halted years ago. Performers in other television shows receive residuals for reruns. Television athletes do not.

Consider the other performer—an actor, for example —who makes a film or videotape appearance; he makes the appearance and receives a residual fee each time his efforts reappear. But the athlete plays the game, and the game is recorded. Excerpts appear on news shows. The game is replayed on tape later in the week. The same game may appear at the end of the season in the "best of . . ." series. It will appear during the off season to reminisce about the past season. It will be played again at the beginning of the next season to prelude the new season. And all for the same fee. Athletes, unite! You have nothing to lose but your place in the Hall of Fame!

The show business of television has expanded into sports so comprehensively that the leagues and the networks are stockpiling films and tapes by the carload. Within a few years it is conceivable that entire new games may be built out of libraries of old games. If it has occurred to this part-time observer, it certainly has occurred to the powers that be.

Or perhaps tomorrow's game, match, bout may be scripted in advance to provide more action and thereby more ratings. Somewhere a young person may be working on a computer to design scripts for an entire season's conflicts so that the games will be far more superior television shows to those we enjoy today.

And when the coach yells for the boys to get out there and win one for the old Gipper, those participants of the future may run out onto the field with the answer, "But it's not our turn till next week's show!"

CHAPTER EIGHT

How to Be
a Star
in the Flag

When you take the time to think about it, and I doubt that you will take the time, the desirability of getting into the act must be of recent vintage. After all, from time immemorial, and even before we can remember, show people were bums. It was not unusual for village fathers to hide their ladies when the wandering players of antiquity came staggering into town. Adulation for the works of show folks may well have been unconfined, but admiration for their lives was highly reserved. They may have been great people to visit but you certainly would not want to admit you lived with them.

They came and they went, leaving behind a trail of broken hearts and deflowered virgins, bilked merchants and disenchanted art lovers. Their visits, however, were not totally destructive; they brought release from the daily monotony and sprinkled a dusting of magic before they left. They were exciting. They were escape. They gave promise that there was more to it all than what was evident.

They sound like our present politicians.

Show people are the closest approximation to royalty that America has ever had, and perhaps because of that fact we retain a gnawing spasm of uneasiness which insists that deep down inside their painted beings they ain't no damn good.

There remains a general distrust and distaste, an insinuation that those show people may still run off with our daughters (and sons), our last slab of bacon, and leave us to the tearful job of reclaiming our soiled children and empty bacon rinds from some disreputable boarding house in Lincoln, Nebraska. But somehow . . . somehow we cannot keep our minds off those people, their shenanigans, their way of life, trick us though they will.

They sound like our present politicians.

The politician. We never trusted him either. Whether vilifying him or applauding him, at least we knew him; he was one of us. He was out of our own milieu; we had cast him into the limelight and we could bring him down again.

The show people were exalted through no doing of ours; they reached their firmaments, their inborn talent propelled in front of us by their native drive. They were managed by people of their own kind who were not from the ordinary dinner-pail world that we inhabited.

But politicians were us and we bloody well knew where they came from. They were not glamorous, they were frequently meretricious, and they lacked any special talent similar to that which caused show people to ascend. To illustrate the changing scene:

In the last pre-television election I was a fledgling radio reporter in Baltimore, Maryland. It was 1948; it was a Presidential election between Thomas E. Dewey and Harry S Truman. The Republic went to bed that election eve convinced that Truman had been turned out by Dewey. At about 11:00 P.M. I approached the Republican national committeeman for the state of Maryland for what would undeniably be the victory statement, a recitation of triumph by the most prestigious Republican official in the state. Think of my personal elation, covering Republican headquarters in a Democratic state, a young reporter, baby face beaming with the achievement of a scoop. The first statement of the high muckymuck of politics and I had beaten every other media man to the draw. I am not conversant with what the rest of the country was doing in those halcyon postwar days, but we had no cluster of microphones which enabled simultaneous statements; it was every man for himself. I had scored an upset for my station comparable to the one Dewey had scored for his party.

My illustrious political virtuoso swept the microphone out of my hand. It would not do for him to speak into the instrument while I held it. He had to feel the pulse of his people jetting through his being as he made the pronouncement that Dewey was carrying the state. He thanked the people of Maryland; he extolled the reshaped virtues of democracy which had Phoenixed from the ashes of the Democrats. He spoke for a minute and a half with fervor, with the taste of that long-sought victory dripping off the ends of his words. He spoke with grandeur. He spoke with the microphone in his ear where he had placed it with the assurance of a man unerringly in control.

We have come a long way since that idiot stuck my scoop in his ear.

With the shrinkage of the power of the printed press and our switch of alliance to the tube, our pundits and politicos have been transferred to television, set in a world of show biz and grease paint and the other contrivances of the information-entertainment machine.

As Americans are prone to do, we abandoned the convenience of our established facilities to pursue the new advance. We are discarders; we have a history of innovation's enforcing obsolescence. We abandoned the railroad for the plane before we realized that they were compatible. Now the years of neglect of the rails will cost us dearly as we attempt to sew a national quilt of adequate, rapid, heavy-duty, non-polluting mass transportation again.

We have bid bye-bye to construction materials and techniques which have been superseded only to find that there was still room for some of the proven methods and materials even though they were no longer number one in the ratings. Other countries—England, France, Germany—have television, but they still retain a lively interest in their newspapers, magazines, radio and forums. Not us. We permitted our fascination with television to shove aside the powers of the other, older media. And now, politics is television and television is show business.

If politics were not show business, politicians would not wear makeup on camera. Lyndon B. Johnson would not have fluffed his hair and tried contact lenses. Richard

Nixon would have a more noticeable beard. Members of both parties would not have to engage coaches to teach them the rudiments of pointing, emphasizing and assuming the stances of fortitude and gallantry before the cameras.

The great misfortune is that we do not admit to ourselves that although you can get TV out of show business, you cannot get show business out of the medium. Show business is showing and telling you something. Business is selling you something. But television has a habit of selling you something while it is showing and telling you something.

Show business uses its facilities to manipulate, to convince, to motivate. When you come right down to it, that almost sounds like a definition of politics. When you can manipulate, convince and motivate simultaneously in every community of a state or nation, electronically, in color, you've got an energy source of boundless impact. As Adam and Eve were prone to say, "It's a world our parents never knew."

There is need, if you are to understand the new politics or are about to become an active participant in the future decision and policy-making of our nation's destiny, for training in the operating mode of the new campaigner. Perhaps as a performer I can be of substantive aid in introducing you to the replacement of the old stentorian style: the new intimate television style.

Let me offer you a gratuitous cram course in self-advancement in politics, adhering to proven principles of show-biz methodology. If any of the following aids are applicable to you, if they can give you some forward thrust in your upward climb, please feel free to adopt them as your own. (If you are auditing this course, please feel free to enter the discussions.)

Before we reach into the heady stuff simmering in the new political cauldron, there is a necessity for a warning. Some of you will already be gifted with whatever it is that allows a human being's personality to "come across" on television. The show-business entertainers who have the metaphysical-psychological something that results in stardom possess the gift innately. The ability to glow from within is inborn. So it is with political entertainers, with men and women to whom the public warms immediately. The wilted word "charisma" is usually attached to politicos, but do not be misled; "charisma" is the synonym for "star quality," the show-business code word for "charisma."

Some of you will have it and some of you will never have it. No amount of training or hard work will give you that star quality. Devotion to a cause, love of mankind—these acquisitions are not substitutes. You either got it or you ain't got it.

The most practical antidote to star quality is the frequent reference to what a great "performer" your opponent is. Dwell on his "performance" whenever possible. Indicate what a great "ad libber" he is, how well "rehearsed" his answers are, how he is always "good box office." Since we are aware that the audience doesn't really trust actors and actresses, and since the general public is not as aware as we that everything on television is a show, you will come off as the sincere one and your antagonist will be tainted with the smell of the grease paint. Only on infrequent occasions should you denigrate your own performances by saying, "If I were as good an actor as he . . . " etc.

The most successful performers are those who know where they are going, who have erected a goal which precludes wasting their time on tangential efforts. So the politically inclined performer must operate, using small gatherings and local functions only as a means for being invited onto television. Once a television platform has been constructed, it must be reinforced and enlarged by frequent appearances for causes which are topically interesting. If the big issue is local housing, talk local housing. If it is anti-busing, talk anti-busing. Until your first elected position (or high appointment) nothing you say will be held against you because you are appearing on television and *nobody remembers what political performers say on television.*

Avoid the newspapers and other printed media in your formative days because the few diehards who still read them will have an unfair opportunity to study your words and ideas. Remember that television broadcast transcripts are difficult to acquire and frequently expensive. Let your opponent make the papers; you make the impression on the tube.

If you do find yourself appearing on TV, try to say nothing conclusive but use charm and conviction to say it. If you are pinned down on issues in the early days of your quest, mention that you covered the subject in so many previous TV appearances that you certainly do not want to be repetitive when there are so many new issues to be faced.

When caught in a situation where you have refrained

from making a statement but one is expected, merely preface your disclosure with "As I have said on TV so many times before . . ." and then inject the new statement.

It is not a catastrophe if you should be quoted in the press as a result of a TV appearance. When people are made aware that what they are reading has been disclosed on TV, they consider it old news and proceed to more personally imperative items.

Have fifty good quotes from reputable, non-controversial heroes—Winston Churchill, Abraham Lincoln, Mark Twain. When you need the ring of authority, attribute the quotes to their originators. When it is an informal appearance, paraphrase the quote into an original thought. Avoid classical references unless you are speaking to professional groups on closed circuit; if you insist on erudition, counterbalance it with a homey aphorism to establish that you do not fancy yourself superior to your viewers.

Live appearances without television coverage are counterproductive. The fact that live appearances render you vulnerable to personal inquisition has unquestionably already occurred to you. If the audience no longer throws vegetables, they can still throw some loaded inquiries which will demand definitive answers.

There are additional pitfalls such as technical malfunctions which can be counted upon to mar your appearances that are live but off-TV. Microphones never work correctly, part of the audience will be unable to see you, the auditoria are either too hot or too cold. The audience will blame you for their discomfiture. When technical troubles plague a TV broadcast, the audience tends to blame the TV station but feels sympathy for you.

The necessity for accepting *any* invitation to appear on TV is proportionate to your place in the scale of recognition. In the beginning, any TV appearance is better than none. We'll concern ourselves about overexposure later on. Some specifics are required here.

Look sincere: Obviously you cannot be sincere and be in politics. When you look sincere, the constituency is assured that you are aggressive, power-hungry, shrewd, pliable, capable of complete reversal—all attributes the voters expect you to call upon for their representation.

Speak softly, looking into the camera as frequently as possible, as if you were gazing into the eyes of a constituent. If you find it difficult to do this, it is obviously not your first election and anything I can tell you will be superfluous.

If it is your first election and you find you are "clutching" when you address yourself to the camera, think of the camera as your mother; talk to the camera as you would your mom. Remember, in the political television world, that camera is your mother since it can give birth to your career or abort it.

Marry advantageously: Your wife will be one of your chief assets not only because of the fulfillment of her function as hostess, but you will be permitted a limited number of wife jokes which will help you deal with subjects you would prefer to avoid. With a smile and a toss of the head in her direction, you can answer a poser with "I'll have to ask my wife about that one!"

Try to remember her name; it's always an endearing gesture for the voters to be included in the family: "Pat (or Mary or Happy) would love to hear your ideas on how we should raise our kids." Make sure that your wife can cry when the occasion demands. Most political wives are so overworked they can be counted upon to cry from exhaustion. But there was an unfortunate woman in an off-year election who lost it for her husband by laughing uproariously when she heard his state chairman had just been stricken by a heart attack.

Have children. Beautiful children are always a boon on camera when the candidate gathers the family around. If your children are not beautiful, send them away to boarding school immediately after your first TV appearance. Prior to this decade it was a godsend to have a large family in campaign work, but the stress of the ecological situation makes two children the mandatory limit for the candidate. If your religious persuasions preclude your controlling the size of your family, your goals in politics are probably of limited scope anyhow. Remember there has not been a President since 1945 who had more than two children in the White House.

Try to have the wife to whom you are married at the time of your campaign be a wealthy person. Television is expensive, and personal wealth is a windfall for the ambitious.

(*N.B.* Because of the increased prominence to which women have ascended in politics, some observations are included for the aspiring political woman performer. Show folks are aware of the old precept "Two stars in the family signals the end of the family." It would be safer if the aspiring political woman were to make her bid at a time when she is married to someone out of politics, a man with a legitimate job. While it is beneficial to have the husband of the candidate in attendance at some of his wife's appearances, the husband should not appear possessively proud on camera. The proud husband reduces you to the level of a playtime candidate, one who is meddling with politics between the car pool and the shopping. Actually, it is necessary that the husband appear only with sufficient frequency to dispel speculation that your ambition is destroying your home.

Women candidates occupy the same relative position in which Catholics, Jews and blacks resided a generation ago; they remind the electorate to be guilty. There is no advantage to be gained by this reminder; it is a hurdle, not a help.

In the matter of costuming for TV, women are under a more stringent code than the men. Dress as if you were going to meet your child's schoolteacher. If you are unmarried or have no children, dress as if you were the schoolteacher. One last warning: Never touch the microphones; they are obvious phallic symbols.)

Catch cold occasionally. All intense campaigners find that they overdo. Catch cold to prove that (1) you are human and (2) you have spared yourself nothing. However, do not succumb to laryngitis, for that makes the TV audience uncomfortable and shows up as a sign of weakness. A cold on camera is a badge of honor; laryngitis is a disability.

Expose but do not overexpose your sense of humor. The late Gypsy Rose Lee was able to arouse as much passion removing her gloves in her later years as she was by stripping totally naked when she was a young performer. It was a Pavlovian reaction called "image"—i.e., a residual vision concocted in the minds of her audience

by her earlier appearances and publicity. The same reaction results from the display of a sense of humor. In the
beginning, nervous tension (and perhaps a sense of
humor) often forces the political rookie to react with a
clever, witty or downright funny line. The television
commentators will implant an image of you from which
you will never escape. You will be funny forever regardless of whether or not you ever again use a funny line in
your quest for power. It is only after you are established,
deeply established, that you can throw a witty rejoinder,
a boffola. I have been in attendance at social occasions
where the Justices of the Supreme Court have been assembled, and although they are secure for life, there is
nothing funny about them.

The late Adlai Stevenson found his brilliant wit a
definite detriment to the acquisition of high office because people missed his salient argumentation waiting
for the punch lines.

Former President Johnson reigned over extremely
serious years, and his humor was evident only after he
left the White House. President Nixon was never inten-
tionally funny.

Lying. It is a paradox of the television era that people
who view politicians on their screens expect them to tell
the truth. It is evidently related to the fact that the
politician is being brought directly into the sanctity of
the home. This is not a purely American idiosyncrasy;
it is applicable to many of the modern nations of the
world. Lincoln might have said, were he alive to see our
political shows today, "You can fool more of the people
more of the time than all of the people in all of the time
before television."

Because you have the advantage of the unexpected, as a political performer you can lie with a great deal more believability than at any time in our history. No one can fully comprehend what you are saying if you construct your speeches with care. As we have noted previously, all too few people read the transcript that the few conscientious newspapers print the following morning. Our present politicians have proven without any conceivable contradiction that it is possible to weave the most fantastic fabric of declarations, predictions and allusions into a security blanket of acceptable rhetoric. It is not the material; it is the performance.

Petite glances of shyness, knitting of the eyebrows, the wide-eyed appeal, the furtive renegade tear, the clutch in the throat, the stance of solidity—the thousand and one devices that actors have used for centuries—are yours to strengthen your presentation of facts that are lies.

Do not become a slave to the styles of the present stars of the power structure; develop your own style. You must learn your own inimitable way of dealing with discrepancies. Most practicable method so far to deal with the exposure of discrepancies is to introduce new discrepancies to cover the old. An adept discrepancy handler can arouse continuing interest for an entire term of office. Never underestimate the advantage to be gained in answering accusations and criticism. Each thrust by your opponent against your credibility can be dealt into a demand for equal time for your own allegations. If you work your deceit skillfully you may end up on television more frequently than the beer commercials.

The debate. There are performers in the political spot-

light who are notorious for their ability to command a
debate. Their numbers are not limited to politicians;
sometimes they are critics or columnists. A performer
inclined to step into the coliseum of combat would do
well to adapt the fast-moving tactics employed by these
polemic-pushers. Ordinarily the purveyors of the kill-or-
be-killed debating technique are the adherents of the
far right and the far left. Liberals, middle-of-the-roaders,
gentle conservatives are lousy debaters. Their lamblike
throats are severed by paper cuts when the spotlight ex-
plodes their combative weaknesses.

Observe the following admonitions and learn to live
with them. If you feel that you are unable to utilize some
of these techniques onstage, perhaps you might consider
ballet dancing or a religious calling.

(A) Remember the audience wants to see a fight, and a
debate is, at least symbolically, a fight to the death. Be
impolite. Criticize your opponent's grammar. Interrupt
as frequently as possible so that your adversary loses his
train of thought. If he does not forget, at least you stand
a chance that the audience will forget. Frequent inter-
ruptions are especially productive when you refer back
to points that have been dealt with already.

(B) Never answer a challenge in a debate. Instead, turn
the challenge to a new point in which you can take an
aggressive stance. Overemphasize the new point so that
the audience thinks that is what you are discussing, not
the challenge. This device may be preceded with the
remark "I'm glad you brought that up," or "I was hoping
you would have the gall to refer to that." After which
statement you derail your opponent.

(C) Make a laughingstock out of your opponent and

take the audience into the joke. Be sarcastic. Then turn to the camera, saying, "Right, folks?" Then utilize the old comedic trick, "But seriously, folks . . ." and proceed into your lampoon.

(D) Feign injured pride, as if your opponent is insulting the intelligence of the audience. If you feel that you are cornered by his comprehensive, correctly compiled facts and figures, use the following statement or a paraphrase of your own: "I'd rather see the problem solved than explained because all these statistics aren't helping *the people*."

(E) Twist your opponent's words. Make it look as if he is overly aggressive. Get him to call you names. Example: Suppose he were to call you a demagogue. Your retort might be "I'm not sure I know what a demagogue is, but I think it's someone who calls people names instead of sticking to the issues."

(F) Never stick to the issues.

(G) Talk into your opponent's time, making it appear as if he is wasting time, that what you have to say is more cogent, more pertinent to the debate. The camera will be on you more of the time, but when it is on him, upstage him with gestures and subtle sight gags to generate snickers and laughter.

(H) Compliment your opponent's staff frequently, your own more modestly. Emphasize that your staff is merely a bunch of volunteers, amateurs untrained in the arts of political expediency, unlike the staff of your antagonist.

(I) Constantly accuse your adversary of doing what you are doing—that is, delaying, interrupting, accusing, lying.

Memorize and utilize these techniques in mock debate sessions and be prepared. I need not ask you to inform me of your progress; you will be recognizable on the tube in the near future.

The politicians inherently recognize the similarity between show biz and their chosen field, but there are some who recognize it more inherently than others. Do such pols rise higher in the hierarchy of government? Don't depress yourself by dwelling on such frustrations. The word "charisma" came into common vocabulary currency only since they put lights, cameras and action on electioneering.

The hope, of course, is that those knowledgeable people who control the destiny of candidates, or the candidates who control their own destiny, are nice people who are disinclined to do bad things to our country, that their quest for power is, at least, in the tradition of fumbling, benevolent Americanism. In which case we may sit back, relax and enjoy their juggling, tight-rope walking and sleight of hand each time their performance season rolls around.

For now we are asking our politicians to be more than public servants. We force them to be parliamentary song-and-dance men. We want to see how they handle an audience; we want to see their wit and charm in prime time, and we want to make a comparison between the way they do their turn and the manner in which the competition performs. We grade them not on their platforms but on their performances, and unintentionally we compare them to our other leading entertainers who appear on the show machine. We are even tolerant of the

appearance of our statesmen and stateswomen on be-
littling comedy extravaganzas. We begin to consider
them performers and show-biz folks to such an extent that
we would rather elect a clean-cut, handsome, glib ad
libber than we would an erudite, intense, stodgy old
poop.

From the point of view of marking an historical beginning, an era when it was evident that the performance was more significant than the material the political
performer was transmitting, the Nixon "Checkers"
speech was a landmark. Threatened by allegations about
the purity of character expected of a Vice-Presidential
candidate, the then Senator came before the public—was
shoved would be more appropriate—to issue a declara-
tion of independence from embarrassing involvement.
Regardless of the merit or lack of merit of the statements,
from a characteristic show-biz point of view it was a hell
of a performance. Any politically motivated aspirant who
did not learn a lesson about the use of television from
that bit of ancient history in TV land will never win an
election for meter maid.

Let the record show that no matter what the record
shows, a politician on television can outperform his real
performance. The past is no longer as pertinent as the
performance.

An observation for political scientists: No fair allowing our officials the indication that they will have a sanc-
tuary in the history of the land. Via tapes and films, we are
amassing the most voluminous archives of public figures
wending their way through the labyrinth of truth and
deception that the world has ever known.

The overpopulation of the future will be enlightened

about the famous and infamous of their past in a way that we can only imagi e as we reel through the films of pre-television days. We have faulty, subjective memoirs to depend on; they will have an unprecedented advantage in being able to read the nuances, the attitudes, the implied and specific benevolence and malevolence in press conferences, off-the-cuff remarks, informal appearances which will comprise the texts of the future.

Foundations have already been devised to compile libraries of audiovisual material which will be available to the scholars and interested parties of the future to provide judicious appraisals of the greatness or baseness of the bygone. Who knows what names will emerge as the basis for cultists to parallel our current aficionados who know Humphrey Bogart and W. C. Fields as gods.

Early American elections were productive of debates where each candidate faced his opponent and ventilated the issues before the public. The debates were held in convenient locations, the press reporting the words objectively to the best of its circulation capabilities. Few of the citizenry saw the candidates; few of the electorate even knew what the candidates looked like or sounded like or how they handled themselves in combat. But they knew what the candidate had said on issues because they read his comments, evaluated his proposals and made a selection that was personally valid. They did not know the candidate, but they were reasonably sure that they appreciated what he stood for.

Once the technological folderol began, the radio, the wire photo, the newsreel, the people had a chance to see more of their candidates, to hear more of them, but they never really knew the impact of their men in face-to-face confrontation until the television debate was hatched.

In that era preceding the television debate, the technique of selecting a candidate was a decisive one. At some point, having done whatever considering he was going to do, the voter clicked a tumbler in the lock of his mind, selected his candidate and never unlocked his decision again. An aspiring candidate could only hope that the voters would delay the locking procedure until the last moment, allowing the newcomer some burst of inspiration, some dramatic information which might shock the lock open again. Otherwise, to unlock the mind of a voter, once it was secured, was almost impossible.

Customarily the voter watched only the progress of his own man. Before the TV debate the viewer treated the appearances of the "other" candidate as just so many commercials for a product in which he had no interest. The decision was made. Then came the first debate.

It was showtime! Close-ups, medium shots, long shots, lighting, attitude, emotional vulnerability, sweating, frowns, smiles, beards, costumes, posturing, stance, ad-libbing, preparation. It was the best show in town that night. It was the last time that issues were ever considered more persuasive than the performance.

The viewers found themselves not only observing their own man but studying the opposition as he sparred and feinted against their favorite. It was not the platform, it was the performance they were studying, and it unlocked a great many closed minds.

From that time on, in political television, stars were born.

There is a lesson that the debates taught the tacticians: A debate is much more advantageous for the challenger. The incumbent, the established star, is allowing the understudy to appear onstage in an equal capacity if he participates in a debate with the challenger. The appearances may have helped Nixon, but they helped Kennedy more.

Suppose, you ask, the debate establishes that the incumbent is so superior a performer to the understudy that the chances for the understudy are destroyed?

There are only two kinds of voters these days in the United States: those who are convinced that their vote alone will win the election and those who are convinced that their vote is a throwaway. The latter are the ones who lock their votes in at the last minute. If the star senses that he has the dramatic capability to destroy the contender, he must take pains to handle himself with seeming humility and compassion lest he establish the contender as an underdog. The last-minute voter, besides being the scourge of the pollsters, is the champion of the underdog.

Since television has forced our political people to attempt to be performers, actors and actresses, to be polished in technique and flawless in audience motivation, we should realize that changes have taken place in the approach of our public personages. For decades politicians have openly "accepted" the aid of professional showmen to theatricalize the delivery of themselves to the nation via TV. The work of Robert Montgomery on the TV appearances of President Eisenhower was perhaps the first avowed use of a dramatic coach for the highest office. Television broadcasters began in 1952 instructing and molding the dramatic capabilities of Congressmen and aspiring political people, and the new era was begun.

The fact that California's Senator George Murphy

and Governor Ronald Reagan were professional actors in no way injured their political careers. What might have tarnished their careers is that some of their political contemporaries were better actors.

What about overexposure, that formidable bugaboo for television performers? More than any other medium that reproduces an image of humanity, television offers to prove the law of diminishing returns. It was Bing Crosby, many years ago, who refused to appear in a weekly television series by saying something like "Nobody wants a person to come into his living room week after week and take over the conversation." Later on, after evidently having forgotten his pronouncement, Bing Crosby appeared briefly in a weekly series which went down swinging. But he was right the first time. Five hundred isn't a bad batting average.

Show-biz people are aware of the necessity for a change of pace to rekindle interest in their act. But the act of a politician consists largely of maintaining an image, not in evincing a razzle-dazzle diversification of talents to endear him in the minds of his viewers.

Nevertheless, TV appearances generate ennui unless the political actor can deliver an occasional unexpected buck and wing. There are few politicians in the history of the show spectacle who have possessed the inventiveness to please the people that Lyndon B. Johnson displayed when he appeared on TV and, for a change of pace, renounced the throne.

An alternative to resigning is predicting larger-than-life events which the public would like to see transpire. If a President can materialize, godlike, on TV and promise the end of a war, an era of peace, the cessation of poverty, the imminent beginning of a non-inflated prosperity, he can wind his audience around his omnipotent finger.

But if a politician's only bit is promises, promises, none of which he delivers, then the viewers will assume that that is his whole act and turn to other reruns when the politico appears to do his number.

The single most unsettling development in the transition from political hacker into song-and-dance man is the estrangement of the politician from his representation. He is becoming as remote as celebrity actors and performers have always been.

Because government seems removed and its officials are now players on the TV screen, the audience—the voters, if you please—is becoming more and more disposed to frustration and discontent. And it doesn't know why. The answer is simple: Our friendly neighborhood public servant has gone on TV and become a star.

The letters that the public writes are used by officeholders as fan mail. In typical television show style, allegedly favorable letters are brandished as popularity ratings, go-ahead signals for the official's latest bit of business. But who's counting the letters? The untouchable star.

Of course only a politician can predict the future, but it does seem as if there will be a preponderance of beautiful-people candidates who look like candidates should look on TV, who can charm their way into your voting machine. We will have considerably increased fan-type interest in the politics of tomorrow. There will be more magazine articles and television shows on the politicians' home life, their romantic indelicacies—a return to the gossipy speculation and ruminations which characterized the golden days of Hollywood. Who can assure us that tomorrow habitués of beauty salons will not be reading *True Confessions from Congressional Sessions* under the dryers?

Somebody ought to tell the public that its role is substantially more than that of the audience or the critic; it is also the role of the angel, the backer, the sponsor. And when an officeholder plays a little too fast and loose in his performance, if the public cannot gets its money back, at least it can change the cast.

CHAPTER NINE

Everybody
Wants to Get
into the ... Movies

According to the latest statistics that I have invented, there are 34,546,839 people in the United States working in "film," studying "film" or attempting to get into "film." "Film" you may remember as the movies, but that is not what we mean by "film" today.

Little old ladies in Golden Age clubs are rushing out to capture the mood and feeling of the social milieu on film. Youngsters in junior high school are soliciting funds so that they can finish their epic production of the life and times of Jean-Paul Sartre. Everybody—social workers, anti-social workers, Ali MacGraw, Joe Namath, my nephew Bruce, the Shah of Iran, Andy Warhol—everybody wants to get into the movies.

"Movies" are film, but not all film is movies. When we refer to movies we are referring to film made specifically for theater release. That they wind up on television is nobody's fault but the accounting department's. To a film maker, the end product is the visual expression of his idea, the communication possible only in a visual medium. He will usually insist that where the film is shown is the last consideration in his mind; all that he asks is that the film be made and shown—somewhere.

It's all because television gave us the screen as a means of expression instead of the word. People think visually now. Thoughts are not expressed; they're illustrated. Television didn't just talk about the weather; it did something about it. It showed it to you. Television didn't just sing or talk about heartburn; it pictured the rust on your piping which caused it.

We really got the picture, inside our homes, away from the darkened arenas in the neighborhood where the previous generation had gotten it. To the sons and daughters, the screen was another window in the home through which they could be entertained as well as informed. From the time they were able to sit up, the screen was showing and telling as well as singing and selling. Film became more than just movies to the kids; film had been their friend and baby-sitter for years.

In the course of their growing up, television was also growing up. A phenomenon occurred to this generation which came of age with television, a first. It was the first generation which saw America as their parents had seen it, as their parents had *really* seen it, through the movies. The same movies. Before the days of television their parents—and the rest of the world—knew America mainly through the movies. Now, with television, the next generation saw the same movies replayed, enabling them to see the concept of the country that their parents had been shown. It was *déjà vu* for the parents, but because of the perspective in which they saw the movies, it was a complete education for the children.

There was little use in telling the kids, "When I was your age . . ." because the kids saw what had been the American Ideal, the dream, the hopes and pretty people who had accompanied their parents through the swamp of the Depression and the jungle of the war years. To the parents, the movies had been beautiful and important and dramatic, an end in themselves. To many of the peoples of the world, including some Americans, those movies had been America.

But the children and the parents discovered truths when they saw those old films via television. The flimsy dramatic quality was revealed to them, and the parents alibied by saying that for intense dramatic impact they had always looked to the stage anyway. They realized that the movies of old had never been an approximation of reality either, because with television they saw the reality of America and the world juxtaposed with movies every day. They learned that even the most realistic American movies had been escapist fare, an entertainment projected in neighborhood dream palaces. The kids played a game about the movies called "Trivia" because they saw the truth—that the movies themselves had been trivia.

As a result of all the finding out, and in spite of the jazzy fanfare, both the adults and their children found out something else—that as industries go, Hollywood and the movies had never even been a significant economic factor in the nation. Goodbye Hollywood.

It had to go; it was not prepared to face the revised role that film had to play as a result of television. Hollywood, which serviced a few thousand theaters in the world on its own terms, was as outdated as the vaudeville it had replaced. If Hollywood had been what the col-

umnists called it, a dream factory, then television was a
reality factory with branch offices in schools, in meeting
halls, in training centers, anywhere that you could set
up a projector to teach, amuse or persuade.

We had brought forth upon this continent a new
generation, the screen generation, and it is conceivable
that they would stand at the precipice tossing over the
old methods of transmitting ideas and watching them
sink while they replaced them with the newer, visual,
methods. There will probably be school television stations and school films instead of school papers and school
magazines. Today or tomorrow the graduating class may
be dumping their yearbooks for the more evocative re-
membrances that a visual cassette may inspire. Can you
imagine seeing those old favorites of high-school or college days not as a dull, lifeless stereotyped class picture
but as a videotape or film? Elspeth Parks and Crazy
Charlie Cohen together again, twenty years from today,
saying, "With fondest memories of Mr. Winkle's class,
here's one for you, Billy, a kick in the . . ." Ah, what
memories! How much more nostalgic than scrawling
epithets in the margins of your yearbook.

There will be a transformation taking place that may
depress those of us to whom the word was always the basis
for the picture. Our heirs may not even realize the significance of the word as they rush forward to get the
picture. Will the future English Literature classes be
studying Sir Laurence Olivier's *Hamlet* as compared to
that of Nicol Williamson—not the words, the film? Will
the kids of tomorrow be griping at the boredom of a
homework assignment that makes mandatory the viewing of an Andy Hardy or Doris Day movie instead of the

reading of Hawthorne or Longfellow or Emerson? Who can say that in fifteen years colleges will not be giving courses in advanced Jerry Lewis or Mike Nichols? Don't wince. Isn't it possible that when they asked the late Anne Hathaway how she regarded Bill Shakespeare's chance for immortality she answered, "Are you kidding! Forsooth, he ain't even good in bed!"

With visual assaults to your sensitivities as a normal bill of fare, there will have to be a change in the movies if they are to fulfill a function. They can never be the "family" medium by definition any longer. The movies that were were movies for the masses—larger audiences, larger expenditures, larger returns, larger losses. If the movies are going to replace the reading habits of the people as well as fulfill the function to entertain, they will be unable to seek their previous common denominator.

The movies that will be will be filmed with ingenuity and inventiveness, by people who are willing to work for considerably less financial satisfaction in return for aesthetic or career satisfaction. There will have to be films of all kinds and, we might as well get used to it, films predicated on the idea that each will find its own audience and that its audience might even be a rather limited one according to our present archaic standards. If a film indicates a small audience, it will doubtless be completed on a small budget. And who knows where the movies of the next decade will be shown, if they will even be shown in theaters? Perhaps the Bijou of the future will be your local cassette lending library or your Cassette of the Month Club.

It is difficult, for those of us to whom film has been

primarily an entertainment, to envision the function that
is forecast for films and videotape in the future. But many
families from one end of America to the other—and in
countries abroad as well—have heard words from a
young boy or girl graduate, words which have brought
chilly shivers to the spine of the family. The words,
"Mom and Pop, I know what I want to do. I want to go
into film."

Let us take the case of Harold Miller, for example.
Let him represent, as much as cultural, ethnic and re-
gional differences will allow him to represent, the youth
questing for a goal in film. He could be your son or
daughter or even you. Convinced that he has found his
occupational preference, having investigated the possibilities of attending a fine film school to become a film
maker, he approaches his mother with his latest aspiration. He is anxious to sound out her opinion of his
ambitions.

She will probably remark as she reaches for her bottle of antacid tablets, "Isn't that cute, my son?" She
has arrived at an age when most mothers and fathers are
anticipating a harvest of pride from the accomplishments
of their children. To Mother Miller, Harold is talking
about movie magazines, the tinsel and the glamor of
Hollywood and multiple marriages and divorces. He is
also talking about a field in which success is for the few
and disappointment is for the mass. He is talking show
business. He is talking madness. O.K. for Jackie Onassis's
child, but not for the Miller child.

"Ma, I don't want to be in the movie magazines. I'm
not sure I even want to be in the movies. I want to be in
film."

"I can see it now," Mrs. Miller laments. " 'Who's that

young buck on Rita Hayworth's arm?' *True Movie Facts.*
'The story nobody knows about Marlene Dietrich.' *Film
Idols.* 'Look out, John Wayne, Harold Miller is coming.'
Are you going to change your name? Do you think your
father and I will have to change our names retroactively,
son?"

"Ma, I don't want to be John Wayne," Harold mutters.

"What's the matter with him? Your father and I have
had many pleasurable hours with Duke Wayne and his
cronies. Presidents like John Wayne. But to tell you the
truth, Harold, I don't know why you want to be John
Wayne. I have you pictured more the Cary Grant type."

"I didn't pick John Wayne, Ma." Harold can see the
futility of continuing the discussion. He decides to await
the return of his father. His father will understand; it is
man's talk anyway.

As his father sheds his hat and coat, Harold pounces.
He explains his intentions to Dr. Miller, tells him of his
heart's desire to go into the field of film.

"Then you gotta go to Europe," Dr. Miller explains.
"Now that we have completely rebuilt them, the Europeans are usurping our pictures. Do you know who makes
the best cowboy pictures? The Italians. Do you know
who makes the best gangster films? The French. Can you
imagine that? Our typical American cowboys and gang-
sters. You know who makes the best horror movies? The
English and the Japanese. I tell you, son, when George
Washington said avoid entangling alliances, he knew
what the hell it was all about."

"But I don't know if movies are—" Harold interjects.

"Do you know who makes the best war movies?" Mrs.
Miller asks.

"Who?" Dr. Miller responds with great interest.

"John Wayne," Mrs. Miller says triumphantly.

Harold shrugs his shoulders and whines desperately, "I just want to make film, to communicate. I want to say something. To be recognized."

"You want to be recognized—wear a name plate that says 'Hi! I'm Harold Miller' like we do at the dental conventions," his father says helpfully, "but first go to college and get a real vocation."

Harold deduces that his parents know nothing about film, that his best course of action is to follow the scholastic path to the university in the area which has a School of Fine Arts leading to a degree in film. The school is of such renown that their curriculum includes Ph.D. work in Bogie and Cagney, Boris and Bela, De Mille and Disney and Looney Tunes.

To the faculty adviser, Harold brings the question of his potential future in the field of film. The adviser is the author of several books on film and the head of the Department of Newsreel and Shorts. He sits back in his director's chair and lights his pipe.

"Depending on the genre that we are discussing, Miller, the film is the wedding of technology and art," the professor professes.

"See, what I want to know, Dr. Sprocket, is whether I can make a living in the field of film. I want to express myself, to be recognized, but I have to eat too." Harold chuckles self-consciously.

"Where else can one freeze the reality of today in the mold of the creator's id? Where else project the future, re-create through the past the display of conscious unconscious, but film?"

"Well, is one prepared to make a living when one

leaves one's studies at the university?" Harold feels compelled to ask.

"We can teach you what articulation in visual terms means, to be vocal though visual, to refrain from the overdoing of your projection through critical analysis of what has gone before."

"Yes, but, Dr. Sprocket, can I leave here prepared—"

"We will turn you out of here with a degree in film that will prove that you understand Eisenstein, Godard, Pudovkin, De Mille and Rosenthal."

"Who's Rosenthal?" Harold asks, to be nice.

"See how you need the work." The professor smiles charitably.

"Do you have any other film makers teaching here?" Harold asks.

"Film makers make films; they don't teach. Teachers teach," the professor answers benignly, implicitly forgiving Harold his stupidity. But Harold proceeds to compound his grossness by asking another similar question.

"Have you," Harold asks, "made many films?"

"I haven't made any films. To be perfectly honest, I'm not ready. I haven't finished my studying yet. I'm only forty-five, but the day will come when I understand enough, when I see the entity as a viable commodity for me. Then . . . then I will make *my* film!"

Harold waits for the importance of the moment to be celebrated before he speaks again. "Well, Dr. Sprocket . . ." Harold begins.

"Yes, Miller, ask it, ask it, that's what I'm here for, Miller." The good professor evidently thinks Harold is going to ask what *his* film is going to be about.

But Harold says, "Dr. Sprocket, I see pictures all the

time at the local movie house that are made by people
who have never been to film school, who come from other
parts of show business or who are the children of stars."

"Listen, What'syourname," Dr. Sprocket says in dis-
gust, "anybody can make a movie. All you do is point the
camera and you make a movie. That's how Rosenthal
made his. But to make a great film you have to have the
talent, the desire, the mental equipment."

"And if I don't have the talent, will you tell me? Will
you say to me, 'What'syourname, you don't have it,
you're wasting your daddy's dough'?" Harold demands
in desperation.

"Well, I have to go lecture now, son. Do you want to
come along and audit my lecture on The Influence of
Religion on W. C. Fields?"

"Dammit, sir," Harold pleads fervently, "when I finish, when I have my degree, can I make a film? What do I
have when I graduate from the school of fine arts in
film?"

"You have, my boy, the ability to enjoy a really good
picture show," Dr. Sprocket says thoughtfully as if he
had never considered it before.

If the scholastic route was not the one for him to tread,
then the world of the daily film maker was the one, he was
sure. So Harold found a Mr. Ernest Charm, the president
of MPMPMP Inc., willing to chat with him about film
companies and their role in the functioning routine of
creating films.

"What we have here," Mr. Charm says, leaning back in
his all-chromium chair which helped accent the rich,
dark tones of his all-Portuguese-cork office, "is the correct
usage of the most complete means of communication.

We don't make feature films. We make industrial films for sales and exploitation of the products of free enterprise. We make training films for the governments, federal, state and local. Publicity films. Solicitation films for charities and foundations. Not a single feature film. Most of the thousands of film companies in business and out from one moment to the next—most of them do not make a feature and don't want to make a feature film. Our business is the business of visual communications, the language of the screen."

"What school of film making would you say you represent?" Harold asks.

"Hah?" Mr. Charm answers. He smooths his fringed leather jacket and peers over his granny glasses at the young protagonist.

"I mean, are you realist, neo-realist, impressionist, what?" Here is the man who can settle the questions plaguing Harold. Here is a man who is making film to make a living making film.

"Harold, we make film to tell a message. We try to take advantage of the fact that a picture is worth a thousand words, to cut through the vagaries of life to the explicit. To really show the things that have to be done and yet we do not discard the lessons of artistry that every one of our predecessors was taught. We may not be artsy, but we are craftsy. We are not interested in wasting time like feature-film makers; we are not making feature films."

"Do you think, perhaps, Mr. Charm, that I could come to work here to learn the business, I mean for nothing, of course?" Harold asks with large diamonds of hope gleaming in his eyes.

"My lad, when you work, you must be paid. A man

who works for nothing is obviously getting what he is worth," Mr. Charm says philosophically.

"Oh, thank you, sir—"

"Unfortunately, my lad, although teaching young people to make films is the thing I would most like to do, we are sometimes in the position where doing the good works we like to do is impossible. You see, what I really want is to make film and film and more film so that eventually we can make enough money so that we can stop doing this kind of crap and make a low-budget feature. Then when we make the money from that low-budget job, I can make the film I've always wanted to make—*my* feature. And then, of course, we can establish our training program. Say, son, where are you going?"

But impetuous Harold is already out of the office.

It is on to Mr. Archer Mangum of Skinflick Inc., producer of sexploitation films. Harold considers being reticent for an instant and then decides that Mangum is making film regardless of the category into which his films slide. The man is making film and a living.

But apparently the man is not making film, because Harold finds the office empty and the name being scraped off the door. Harold is informed by the paint-scraping person that Skinflicks Inc. is now Skintapes Inc. and the change has necessitated a move to larger and more electronically versatile quarters.

But it is the same Mr. Mangum. "Lemme tell you something, kid," Mr. Mangum responds without being asked, "tape is in. Videotape is gonna be film soon, I'm betting on it. We are experimenting with a system of taped nudies that is going to make the old films look like a religious show. You know anybody with money who wants to make a fortune, send him to me. I'll make 'em rich. You got any money, kid, any nest egg—I could make you rich. How about your father?"

"No, see, Mr. Mangum, I thought if you could let me start in—"

"That's the thing, kid. That's what we did. We invented a system. Well, it's almost perfected; it's not quite right. You sure you ain't got no money?"

"No, see—"

"Kid, listen to this. What's been the main problem with porno and skinflicks and specific sex films? I'll tell you—expense. The actors cost. Now Molly and me figured—"

"Who's Molly?" Harold asks.

"Molly, my wife. Now Molly and me figured if we could produce a stag film with one person in it, we could cut the price. But if we could produce a stag tape using laser beams and holographs so that when you buy one of our set-ups you can project the sex partner in 3-D right in the room! Get it, kid, get it? That way, when you are having your fantasy, you could have your fantasy! Miraculous?"

"I didn't realize that you can do that with laser beams and holographs. I know the cassette people are working on something, but—"

"Kid, a whole new world is opening up. Laser beams may help in the curing of terminal diseases, they may help guide airplanes, and they may help Molly and me do the one thing we always wanted to do." Mr. Mangum points to the nude woman posing for the provocative videotaping in the adjacent studio. "With this-here stuff we hope to get a little money together so that we can get out of this rat race. The skin business is getting too crowded. There's too much product; it's overpowering the lust. So we'll get the money and get out of this miserable business altogether."

Harold is diverted, watching the lovely actress go through her paces. "Hey, kid, don't worry, as soon as Molly is finished posing I'll introduce you. Yessir, we're going to pack it all in, we're going to take the money and make *my* film. None of this artless shit, *my* film."

Mangum proves to be correct, at least in part, in his assessment of videotape and its imminent invasion of what has been the exclusive domain of film. There were TV production firms who were electioneering for the complete use of videotape as the medium for their medium. But there were other voices who were shouting that tape had an even greater future for use away from television. In shows, in theaters, in night clubs, there were videotape freaks who were experimenting with tape instead of film. Although tape was not as useful when it was projected—it lost fidelity in blow-up—it had immediacy and portability.

Harold sought out one of the young tape groups who were roaming the city, videotaping with portable equipment, which was almost as feasible in its versatility as Super 8mm camera equipment. The video radicals were displaying their wares in tape festivals for pennies, in the same way that young actors worked for the joy of performing or young film makers worked just to make films.

Harold found his tape group at a small downtown coffeehouse called Video-Cityo, where, under the direction of a young man named Groovy Baby-Doll, the group was displaying its latest tapes. After a showing which lasted about an hour, Harold sought out Mr. G. B-D. to ask if there were any openings in the company. Mr. G. B-D. was dressed in overalls, a lace undershirt, red and blue shoes and a set of earrings, both on the same ear.

"I don't know if I understood what you were saying," Harold confided, "but I think I would like to learn the business with you folks."

"Mother, you're really into it. You dig tape, and you are seeing the living end when you see tape. Instantaneous! A gas to edit. The processing scene is a wild one because it don't happen, man; tape is, you don't develop it. And it saves bread. Shit, man, tape, you can really swing with it."

"I really did dig it," Harold agreed, eager to please, "but in your presentation here, I think you were trying to tell the frustration of city life and the futility of trying to cope with the population explosion. Right?"

"Shit, mother, you didn't dig my number at all. I'm telling about me, about my hatred for the established flick fuckers. The people who make the films. Don't you see it, man, the way they make films for the money? They are shitting the public all the time, doing what they want and not giving the public what it wants. Never giving me what I want. Me! I want to see flicks for me! My tapes say to them, screw film! Tape is here and it gives you instant satisfaction."

"Then you feel tape is it!" Harold shouted, caught up in the devoted dedication of Mr. G. B-D. "Take me along, Mr. Baby-Doll. Let me swing with your group to help you serve!"

"Bite ass, you mother," Mr. G. B-D. said. "We can't

afford no learners leaning on us. This group is on its way. Man, we will use our tapes to penalize and pulverize the world. We will show the world how they are getting nothing from the film makers but horseshit. We'll blackmail the film people into giving us bread to lay off. Then when we got the bread! When we got the bread . . ." The man had a look of absolute, sheer ecstasy. Harold worried a little about him, as if the man were about to be transported to some great tape studio in the sky. But Mr. G. B-D. suddenly looked down at Harold and said, with great meaning coming through the delivery, "Then, when we got the bread, we can make the flick that we have always been digging. *Our* flick, mine. Where I tell where it's really for me. Me! Me!"

Harold figured that the answer, simply translated, meant that there was no position available.

It was good fortune that Harold went to the headquarters of Rice Whizzers, the cereal for the young at heart. Why did he go to a cereal company? He went to the cereal company because they had just announced an investment of several million dollars in feature films. The president of the company, who was hardly older than Harold himself, had acquired the company in a stock manipulation which earned him the cereal company, an automobile muffler firm and Park Place in exchange for the only American firm manufacturing handcuffs and casket handles and another holding company that owned the air rights to Miami Beach.

"Why are you investing in films if you are a cereal company?" Harold asked the youthful tycoon, Mr. Farina.

"Because film is there. Because movies are better than ever and because the returns on a successful film are better than you can get from investing in other kinds of products. There is also no industrial turmoil such as you have when you own capital goods. With a film, your employee-employer relationships end with the end of the film. You lease all of your equipment and disband your organization after the film is over. It's something they never learned out in Hollywood. You don't even need a place of business."

Harold looked at Mr. Farina with respect. "Well, if you find that this is successful, will you give up the cereal business and really make films or will film always be a sideline?"

"If it is successful," Mr. Farina answered, "as it will be because everything that I touch turns to gold, I will probably take a year off—"

"And make *your* picture," Harold finished for him.

"If you're so smart, why aren't you rich like me?" Mr. Farina asked, countersigning a note for the Bank of America.

"I thought anybody could make a film, Harold," Harold's father remarked when the prodigal returned home to refurbish his pocketbook and his stomach.

"Everybody is making films," Harold responded gloomily, making short shrift of a mess of pottage his mother had placed before him. "There may not be any Hollywood, but the decentralization makes it harder, in a way, to get into the business. Everybody is so self-indulgent, all they can see is their film, what they want to say."

"But you said that the theaters are crying for product. You said that TV is gobbling up the film faster than anyone can supply it," his father puzzled. "How do you intend to get into the business?"

"I guess I can start at the bottom, trying to find a working company that will let me sweep the floors and then move up the rungs of the ladder of production. Editing, assistant director, assistant producer—everything until I can get to the part I want to get to and then I can make *my* film."

"But, Harold, how about . . . how about if you start at the top?" the older gentleman asked cautiously. "If you get the required amount of money from somewhere, you can make your film right away."

"Are you offering?" Harold sobbed, dropping his spoon into his mess. "You know, movies can be made anywhere from seventy-five thousand on up, depending on what you want to say in the film and how you say it."

"Well, that's what I figured," the older generation said with a sigh. "Well, I am prepared to give you the money to make your picture."

"Oh, my daddy!" Harold wept.

"But not quite yet," his father continued. "You see, I have to make enough money at dentistry so that I can stop for a while. Then, as soon as I can do that, I can sit down and write *my* book. And from my book . . ."

CHAPTER TEN

Everybody
Wants to Get
into Records

Listen, darling, they're playing our song. Is that our song, darling? What is that—is that a song, darling? What are they playing it on? And frankly, darling, look at the musicians. What are they?

Where have they all gone, the big bands, the vocalist who sang with the band, your penny loafers and brown and white saddle shoes? All is gone. But all is not lost, darling. With everything becoming part of the big reality show, it was too much to expect that our broadened horizons would allow our music to stay the same. We have come a long way since the dear recorded days beyond recall when it was enough to sing only about love.

We had explored every crook and crevice of our emotions concerning wanting and longing and needing and waiting and hoping and missing and seeing and crying and dying and trusting and feeling and laughing and saying, and meaning and not saying, and saying but not meaning, and thinking but not saying, and saying and be-

ing sorry, and being sorry and not saying, and wanting to
say but not saying, and wanting not to say but not being
able not to say, and asking but hoping not to be answered,
and hoping not to be asked, and hiding and crying, and
hiding the hoping, and lying, and trying not to lie, and
echoing and re-echoing, and smiling through crying, and
crying inside and laughing outside, and—it was enough
already. It was all we dealt with in our "popular records,"
the care and feeding of love.

The American popular recordings market was built
on the packaging and selling of love. The European
music-makers covered more varied fields of endeavor in
their records. They were concerned about storytelling,
who did what to whom and why. They would just as
soon sing a little ditty about the high cost of living under
the present regime as moon, June and spoon. They
would also include a few little chants about illicit affairs,
would-be illicit affairs and romances that we would not
even talk about, let alone put to music. What they were
really doing was editorializing.

While we were Juneing and mooning, they were singing about the things that bothered them. If they produced a memorably lovely piece of music that was imported to the U.S., the lyrics were translated back into
some kind of activity that accompanied love. Even one
of the great World War II songs, "Lili Marlene," the
story of a whore-lady under her lamplight, on translation
became the pallid tale of a gingham-gowned cheerleader
awaiting the return of her boy friend, the preacher's son.

In the old countries it was different. The people lacked
the proliferation of media that we had where free expression was encouraged. Some of their best songs

emerged from the cabarets, those petite night spots that featured politically scathing revues masquerading as entertainment. We probably needed the catholic and bland type of stuff we were doing because our music and recording business was pure show-biz entertainment.

There were a great many Americans editorializing and complaining in music, but we tried not to notice them. They were rhythmic, we told ourselves, they were quaint, we assured ourselves, and they were happy and placid, we deceived ourselves. And they were telling us that they were black and singing the blues. There were brothers who were white who were also singing about their troubles in the dust bowls, in the poverty pockets and the railroad sidings. But the recording business was a commercial enterprise, based in New York and Hollywood, and selling happiness, so most of the editorializing in the nation's music went unrecorded. The record business, like the film business, offered escape and blue skies all the way.

The advent of television, following so closely the upheaval of World War II, activated a couple of momentous changes. First, radio, as we have seen in this very book, assumed a new role, one much more closely dependent on music, but it was recorded music, because live music was far too expensive to be a staple diet of the wireless. Then there was the technological revolution: the introduction of the microgroove records which had been perfected as a sideline of war research. The toppling of the 78 rpm dynasty by the high-fidelity 33 and 45 records was more of a revolution than any of the improvements that followed. Stereo, tape, four-channel stereo—whatever effect they had seemed less of an innovation than the introduction of the long-playing records. Apparently people began to expect progress as a logical commercial sequence of events.

What made it so easily acceptable, this progress, was the affluence of the times. The new things that were put on the market were issued and owned. New records came out and we could afford to rush out to the neighborhood diskery and buy them if we liked.

Especially if we were young. Contemporary popular music is largely an innovation of the young. Their tastes and lack of tastes were the determinants for the direction such music would take. Prior to the television generation music that expressed the gurglings of dissatisfaction, of dissidence and of injustice was largely confined to live presentations, rallies, meetings, picket lines. The only thing we were recording for mass consumption was the music of love.

Then television did its reality bit. It brought the faces of real people into the home along with the trained professionals. Faces and places that most of the parents had never known, let alone that the youngsters had never known. The parents had grown up on words of news with an occasional dramatization, "The March of Time," "Five-Star Final," re-creations of the news. But the TV generation grew up on the news starring all those formerly invisible people coming in all shapes and sizes and ideologies and colors, coming to tell their troubles and to show the youngsters what was going on.

And what the youngsters saw was certainly real enough to them: films of fighting and dying and hating and pleading and burning and lying. Then, right next to that, they saw the glossy commercials for the products of the "good life." There it was, side by side for the young people to see, the bad and the beautiful, the real and the gloss. The youngsters, horrified as all young people have been for all time at the complaisance of their parents, rejected the whole TV picture.

They rejected the standards of commercial banality that their parents had learned to live with; they rejected the commercial sounds that appealed to their elders. They rejected the trained voices, the structured harmony of the current favorites; they rejected the precise instrumentation of the sounds that their parents had been hearing.

The wanted reality, the kids; they wanted sounds that sounded like themselves and the real people they saw and they were certainly not going to get them in the svelte music of the available recordings. Apparently they wanted amateurism because they were seeing amateurs, and they identified themselves as amateurs.

So little Johnny and Mary went into show business themselves. They started a rush on the instrument market that had never been seen before. They bought guitars and wooden flutes and bongos and drums and they started listening to the music that real people were putting down. Every block had its own weird assortment of youngsters who were making up a rock group. Wherever you looked there were four kids, a guitar and a cigar box making music. Everything was a "group."

And what were they singing about? They used the music to express themselves, their dissatisfaction with the way things were going in the United States. They were singing about what was bothering them in the same manner as those Europeans had been singing about the

things distressing them. The young people were singing in a vocabulary peculiarly restrictive, so their elders
could not understand, about subjects that they knew
their elders did not understand. They sang about drugs
and they sang about conventions that were rigid without
reason and they sang the blues that they learned from
the blacks and the poor and the soldiers going out to the
strange Pacific Involvement we had acquired. They were
editorializing all over the place with their new guitars
and their amateur arrangements.

Politically speaking, the young people seemed to be
non-persons. The ones who conformed to the standards
of the adults were blending in and the others just seemed
to be having a good time, a-picking and a-singing and
sharing and talking L-o-v-e for everybody in addition to
love for one another.

The recording companies, Mr. Columbia, Mr. RCA,
Mr. Capitol, Mr. Decca, Mr. Mercury, Mr. Etc., continued to release what they had been issuing without
realizing what was going on. What was going on was the
kids' insistence that they were not interested in "stars"
doing professional renditions. They wanted to do it
themselves, a kind of rebirth of the old days when the
folks sat around the piano or uke and sang.

It was almost uncanny how widespread this youth
movement in music seemed to be. Worldwide. They
were beating the drums and picking guitars and sharing
each other all over the world, in different languages, but
somehow better able to understand than their elders.

And then they began to make their own records.
Young entrepreneurs recorded themselves or their
friends and the little labels were flitting around the

country like butterflies, lighting first in this city or that, to establish an occasional hit. The names of the groups were usually picked for their shock value, until finally they ran out of shock and just tried to be outrageous or unique. The funniest thing about the records besides the experimental sound was the names that the "artists" picked. After a while, of course, the names became so unusual that they sounded usual. When everybody's crazy, everybody's sane.

Simultaneous with the "off label" marketing came some redoubtable surveys which shouted that the teen-agers really had quite a preponderance of money to spend. The way the media, the publications had it, every teen in America had an income of $10,000; more money was in the hands of the non-voters than in the hands of widows and mutual-fund handlers, and those kids were spending this money with inspiring alacrity. They may not have been buying records by the outstanding estab-lished stars, but they were buying something.

"Attention, America," the record companies shouted. "Attention, listen to the voices of your children! Atten-tion should finally be paid to such music and such money!"

"You call that music?" the parents queried when they heard the plaintive mewling of their little people. It was the same way their own parents had shouted, "Turn off that goddam noise!" when *they* heard the big-beat sounds of Benny Goodman and Tommy Dorsey.

Mr. Record Company bought out the young entre-preneurs or hired them to replace his own vice-presidents who were over sixteen and balding. But as quickly as they bought out the small companies, new ones opened.

Where there had been five or six major companies there
was a record company in every empty store and nobody
cornered the market. It was the best of all times for the
young; it was the worst of all times for the big companies.

The sound that the record companies were looking
for was the sound of money that came from the money
sound, the music for which those reputedly rich teen-
agers would shell out the shekels. If the kids wanted songs
about drugs, they put out songs about drugs. If the kids
wanted to slam a war, knock their parents, or praise free-
loving, the record companies complied and put out those
records. Those companies knew too much to keep guessing and losing, to keep issuing flops that did not take into
consideration what the teenie millionaires wanted that
week, so they went so far as to take their companies where
the authentic sounds were being born. They decentral-
ized their operations, those big companies, moved their
recording studios to the heartland of music—to the
South, the hinterlands. They begat the Nashville Sound,
the Memphis Sound, the Motown Sound by constructing
huge facilities at the spots where the music that was
making it was born.

But the companies worried a great deal about the
shelves. That's not a rock group, the shelves; that's the
warehouse shelves which had a tendency to pile up with
records that never in this world would be sold. The pro-
duction-line technique they had perfected had broken
down because as soon as they caught on to what the young
people were doing, the fickle young were off to another
mood, another dance, another idea. It was nerve-wrack-
ing for the companies; executives arrived and departed
like 747s. If it was unpredictable for the companies it

was panic for the recording groups, because as soon as a group was popular, spent its income for suits and immense posters of itself, it was dropped from the heights by the fans and it was back to obscurity. For the recording artists the record business was a roller coaster, up and down and then, frequently, out. They became collectors' items immediately because most of them never made a second record.

So the record companies began to manufacture amateurism. Realizing that the kids wanted the amateur sound, the sound of unpracticed reality on vinylite, they started to form groups to give the kids what they wanted. The record companies retooled their assembly lines and started to manufacture amateurism; they had trained, professional neophytes. They formed fresh groups to give the kids what the kids were looking for in the unpracticed, good-time sound.

The companies had no teenage scruples to guide them in their religion, the quest of money. As soon as they could detect any kind of trend in the taste of their consumers, they created non-existent groups, non-group groups. What the young people thought was a group called the Gargles was really the same four people who had recorded the prior week as the Sniffles and, in fact, was really the same four people who had won a gold record for their million-seller "Scrubadoogee" as the Headaches. Four or five professional singers, moving around an octave or two, an arrangement or two, and electronically enhanced could sound just a little different, mostly the same.

Actually, all of the records were electronically manipulated; no singer sang without an echo chamber, no group worked without overdubbing. Overdubbing is the process where a singer or an instrumentalist re-records his voice or instrument over the previous recording until the record sounds like more than one voice or instrument. There was a story making the rounds that only one musician really worked in New York and that by careful overdubbing he was able to play all the parts in all the records for the whole year. I know it's not true because I made it up. There really were three of them.

The record business was a business like sports. If recording artists didn't sell, they were traded or released the way low-average athletes are abandoned. One of the non-performers in the sales-department charts was classical music. Classical recordings, always a consistent but slow seller, began a severe fall from grace. Never forgetting for a minute that classical music has a cultural value and is part of the artistic heritage of music, the recording companies promptly forgot it. The output of classical recordings of new aggregations or ensembles dwindled to a trickle, one company going so far as to issue old recordings in forms such as "Beethoven's Biggies" and "Tchaikovsky's Goldie Oldies." The recordings of the classic pieces were assumed largely by foreigners even though America probably has the best symphonic orchestras in the performing world. But if you think about it, all those old-time guys who wrote that music were foreigners anyhow.

Many of the top rock singers and groups were foreigners. The companies did a bigger importing business than the foreign-car dealers. Those foreign acts loved to work the United States; they could make more here in a brief time than they could anywhere else in the world, and TV appearances made them overnight local stars in America.

Those essential TV appearances by the recording stars proved as problematical as powerful. Since most of the "hot" recordings had been electronically enhanced, the live repetition of the number by the group produced a colossal disappointment. The curtains parted, the spotlight hit the stage as the MC's voice reminded the viewers of the greatness that was about to regale them. The group came flying out to spread their musical virtuosity to their waiting fans and what happened? Their unaugmented little voices and their vapid instrumentation dribbled out across the air.

Many of the groups were unable to demonstrate the basic techniques of crowd-pleasing because they had not been trained to perform. They had never had the seasoning, the time, to learn how to move and how to look graceful in front of their admirers.

On their appearances, some of the groups, some of the singers would mouth records, moving their lips to the recorded version of the song to give the effect that they were doing the number. The young people accepted it briefly, but youth had been clamoring for credibility and such a system had to be a loser. The TV stations and the recording companies did not object to those pantomime performances; the TV stations did not have to pay performing rates and the recording companies had the advantage of having the recording heard in unblemished version without disappointing those avid young people.

The imported groups fared somewhat better. The English rockers and the Australian swingers were, after all, the cream of the crop, the best of the new, the pick of the litter. Those who came here were already big there, wherever *there* was; they knew how to move and how to blend in with the audience and draw them into the act if need be. They had been through it before.

The TV-viewing youngsters, veterans of thousands of hours of simulated stimulation, cultured in show biz, had become critics with a threshold for professionalism that was far lower than they knew. They wanted amateurs but they didn't want them to be *that* amateurish. The young audience ended up by lionizing the new performers who could get up there and put on a show, the performers with technique, those who had—heaven help us—talent. They set up their own star system which practically paralleled the one their parents had set up before them.

And don't tell the parents that they began to enjoy some of the new music as well as their kids did. The financial figures showed that not all of the new records were bought with the grubby dollars of teenagers. Many of the recordings were bought with the grubby dollars of their elders. The radio stations which were particularized as "bubble gum" stations swore that some of the bubble gum was being mashed by listeners with false teeth. The adult taste was influenced by the millions of transistor radios and phonographs blaring out the latest hits. The parents could not help tapping their toes to the music—discreetly, of course, but tapping away, nevertheless.

The Beatles began sounding better, the parents agreed, and wasn't it a shame they disintegrated? And Sinatra, before he retired, tried a few Rod McKuen easy-rider ditties, and Mantovani moved three squares forward to music that Perry Como might sing.

And Ed Sullivan, until the last show, kept on introducing groups which were familiar to young and old
when he said, "A really, really great group you all will
enjoy, The Law and Order." And even Ed knew what
we all must know secretly—that the big bands aren't
coming back.

CHAPTER ELEVEN

Show Biz
and the
Business Show

You don't believe that everybody is in show business; you don't think that the world has developed into a cast of billions. The effects of this mutation may not be evident to you because you are not making a film, a record or a broadcast. You might simply be involved in your day-to-day living, carrying on your workaday processes, having categorized yourself as a no-harm-intended lay person.

There is a sinister revelation awaiting you—you're in candid commercialism. There is singing and dancing and selling going on all around you, and although you are not aware of it, show business is being perpetrated on you. It is being foisted upon you. The business show, the industrial show.

This hidden area of sell-entertainment may be the second largest branch of show business in America. The custom of presenting industrial shows has been exported to some of our friendly overseas countries. But there is no way of knowing how much money is spent putting on industrial shows, the shows for insiders, the shows that never play the theaters, the tents or the open market.

The industrial show is a show that is intended to sell the sellers (that definition will be clarified later). Some of the shows are full-blown extravaganzas, and some are insignificant puffs meant to introduce a new item or a new line of merchandise or service. The shows are formulated by a shadowy group of producers who are unknown to the general public—and the show-people public, for that matter.

These producers circumvent the normal production facilities, often avoid the use of union performers and technicians. They have produced hundreds of big-time shows, none of which has ever played Broadway or any Main Street in the land.

The immense talent agencies are rarely involved in the industrial shows; big-name talent is not featured in the casts. The shows may originate in New York or Los Angeles or in the city where the company manufactures its product.

Some of the productions are staged with such grandeur and intricacy that the audience must be brought in from all over the country rather than move the show around. In the good years when business is affluent and hopeful, the shows are bountiful and splendid. In bad years, along with all the other promotional apparatus, the industrial shows go down the drain.

The "Chevy Show," a production which introduced the new car models for the year to dealers throughout the country, was reputed to have cost a million dollars This cost included the show, a complete, original musi-

cal comedy and the transportation of the show to four
or five locations convenient for the assembly of all of the
dealers in the country. The dealers were then wined,
dined and oriented for the coming season's beauties and
prices. (Prices slightly higher west of the Rockies.) When
those Chevy dealers left the show, they were full of gas
and vinegar and ready to sell cars.

Not all of the industrial shows are Broadway-caliber
productions or even road-show versions. The ingenuity
depends on the money spent and the producer himself. It
is an amorphous chunk of show business which caters to
a non-critical, non-paying audience of which you may
be a part.

For the reason that you might never be able to go
backstage to know this world without a personally con-
ducted tour, I am going personally to conduct your tour.
The people you meet are compilations because I would
rather clutter your mind with generalities than actualities. Generalities may be inaccurate, but actualities sue.

Bernie Wartheim's office is in one of the newer office
buildings on Park Avenue in New York. The well-
appointed and efficient motif is as indicative of success as
the display of awards which he has accumulated in the
recent past. Wartheim is the winner of the 1968 SARAH
(Society of American Retailing Honorarium), the 1965,
1966 FANNY (Award of the Foundation and Brassiere
Manufacturers) and the 1967, 1969 Oil and Petroleum
Industry Salute. Wartheim himself must be a man in his
late fifties, flamboyant and full of energy. His gray hair is
worn long and well coiffured. He has just an admirable
trace of a Hungarian accent. He can best explain indus-
trial-show philosophy.

"Do you know what it is Wartheim is?" he asked. I told him that I wanted to hear it in his own words. "Well, mein boy, Wartheim is with the greatest drama of all, the theater of commerce, the biggest theater in the country. I am David Merrick of the industrial shows. I sell the sellers. You understand what I am telling you? Everybody wants Hollywood, Broadway. Not Wartheim. I do maybe ten big shows a year—ten! Big shows. Big budgets. Original music, original lyrics. Original scripts. Writers write. Actors act. But not an agent agents to Wartheim. What a wonderland!

"I am getting the money from the industry itself to make shows like in the big-time. There ain't no show business like this behind the Iron Curtain. I can tell you —don't ask! Look." Wartheim picked a script from his desk. "Look at this, music and dancing for the telephone company. The Yellow Pages. Not for the advertisers but for the people who solicit the advertising. To inspire them to sell the advertising in the pages!"

Wartheim began to sing some of the lyrics from the songs in the script. "If your mouth don't do the talking/ *You* and not your fingers will be walking. Sell the hell out of Yellll-ow Pages!" He showed another script. "Here's one we do for the Bank of New York Drive-In Tellers. We even got in this one a car on stage to show the technique of how to get them to bank better by this bank, in song and dance. Here's another one for the Black Flag bug-killer salesmen.

"It's what television has done. They sell the public everything from polishes to pollution on TV, from bread and butter to diseases. The public runs out screaming, I want that! I got to have that! I need that! But the salesmen don't know nothing about it. Here come the crowds yelling! He stands there. What does he know? Nothing! They ask a question. He can't answer. They ask another; he can't answer. They go home. He can't go home because he has lost his home and his job.

"You got to sell the sellers. You got to fire the man up who distributes. The man on the street who sells to the retailers."

I found myself gazing at the man with ingenuous wonderment.

"You are gazing at me with ingenuous wonderment? Picture this scene in your delicately facile mind. A man— let's call him Louis—turns out in Detroit the New Louie V8. It's a new car he is turning out every year for the obsolescence market in America. It's expected that he turn out a new car to make his last new car old already. Right? Now he's got to sell the car to the public, so he takes it out ads in the television, the radio and the printed places. 'The New Louie! Bigger than the old Louie, more comfortable than the old Louie. A Louie you couldn't go without it!' You got it so far?"

"It's called advertising," I said gingerly. I had him.

"Not a question of the world, you're right!" Wartheim sat back and made a steeple with his fingers. "How do the public get its advertising? We know how. It gets it in show-business form. In a show it's a commercial; the commercial itself is a show, and the audience is tickled enough or something enough to want to say to itself, 'I got to have that new Louie.' Right?"

"It's advertising." I was stalwart.

"I'm not arguing," Wartheim shouted. "But it's show business that is carrying the advertising. The people expect to see commercials in their shows. They expect to see selling in their shows. Remember that. Everybody sees show business all day in this country. Ford is in show business, gasoline is in show business, doctors and lawyers is in show business. There's a potful of selling dropped into the show business in this country. People expect it, but what happens at the point of sale? Hah?"

"What happens?" I asked.

"All right, now watch this carefully. So far we are talking general public. But Mr. Louie has got to get the cars out to the point of sale, to his dealers. What is the Louie dealer saying to himself? 'Oho!' he is saying, 'here comes it another lemon to sell when we just got barely out of last year's Louies.' Mr. Louie, the manufacturer in Detroit, he knows that. He got to fire up the Louie dealers from coast to coast with the enthusiasm to sell the cars Louie is turning out like pizzas in Detroit.

"But Mr. Louie knows something else. He knows that the Louie dealers, like everybody else in America, is used to show-business selling. What does he do? He makes up should be a show to sell enthusiasm, to sell happiness, to sell the goddam new Louies to the Louie dealers. Before the car even gets to the public, he got to get the cars into the showrooms.

"He hires Wartheim. He says to Wartheim, 'Make up a show for the dealers in my Louies. Make singing and dancing tell them what is so great about the new cars. Make up a show should enthuse all the Louie dealers and make those boys eager and ready to throw the Louies at the public. A little excitement, a little sex, a little music to introduce this year's new Louie couldn't hurt. A nice show, we'll take it across the country and bring the Louie dealers and their wives to the show. We'll have a party, we'll have drinks, we'll fill those sonofbitches full of happiness; they'll march out singing the Louie Song for the Year and they'll place orders so I ain't left with a single pizza.' In other words, for the general public there's some selling dropped into the show business; for the dealers, there's some show business dropped into the selling.

"And it's the same for a thousand and more products turned out in this country. They make up an industrial show to sell the people in the industry. The girdle and bra manufacturers show the new line with music and dancing and drinks and pretty little pussycats. The banks and branches to give a pep talks. More money is spent on industrial dramas than on the professional shows or theaters in this great country. And that's because you can't get people to do anything anymore without a little song and dance."

"Well, I would like—" I ventured.

"You would like, you would like. I know what you would like. You would like a job. You would like Wartheim to cast you in a show like the one I am doing for the Dairy Association. You would like to be a dancing bottle of milk to tell the dairies across the country that milk is still good for you even if maybe it's got a few things in it from the grass that could be a surprise in a test tube. Then I got a scene in there . . ." Wartheim's eyes glazed ever so slightly as he mentally exited and began to envision his new masterpiece. "Where the cow sings 'Moooo-re profits for you-oooooo if you can doooooo what the consuuuuuuu-mer wants. Sell her juuuu-ice, sell her caaaake and anything to make an extra buck or twooo.' Oh, what a winner this show is going to be!"

"Sounds great. I—" I tried again.

"You know," Wartheim crackled, "that Milliken gets

up a new show every year and it costs them about a million dollars. *That's* show biz! If I could get that one—just once! And I should because I am the Sol Hurok of—"

"Well, suppose I wanted to—" I picked up quickly.

"Suppose, suppose. You suppose you could star in a hotsy-totsy extravaganza like the General Motors, the Milliken! You think Coca-Cola, Pepsi-Cola, Any-Cola would let an amateur like you fall on your face on their money? You think we don't get reviewed? You think because the newspapers and the magazines and the TV don't give us three stars or three bells we ain't big-time?

"Look at my notices from *Women's Wear Daily* over there." He flung his arm grandiosely in the direction of the wall. There were notices from *Women's Wear Daily*, from the *Journal of the American Medical Association* for his show pointing out the evils of socialized medicine in some countries. There were pictures of Wartheim and Dr. Teller, Dr. Heller and Mitch Miller. There were golden records and plaques and scrolls.

For purposes of investigation and to make sure that he didn't sing me any more songs, I asked Wartheim, "Who else does industrial shows?"

"Oh, you're not even in a position to hire and you're dickering. Listen to this—" He began to sing a lilting thing, the lyrics of which concerned a leading headache remedy and the desirability, for the druggist, of placing it on the front of the shelf. One of the stanzas he particularly enjoyed because he launched into it with great gusto: "If you kick that aspirin to the back of the shelf/ you'll get a little kickback yourself! / Tax exempt!"

Without the slightest encouragement he proceeded to demonstrate one of the dance steps which accompanied the song, indicating that the headache remedy shoved plain aspirin off the shelves and out of the stockroom. I was motivated to stock a gross.

"You know who wrote that?" Wartheim asked, out of breath from his performance. I stopped applauding long enough to inquire who. "Roger Mitchell. Yes, don't look surprised. The same Roger Mitchell who wrote *Love-flower Blooming* on Broadway last season. A flop maybe, but Broadway. He's got two wives and four children. He's got a mistress and a mister. He needs money. He did the low-calorie-seltzer show for me, the no-bra bra revue, and he did the carpeting show. The music was written by Bill Brouning and the book by Carole Coleman, who did *Wall Street by the Numbers*."

"Boy, that's some line-up!" I marveled. And well I should have marveled because the talent alone was worth a fortune, or it would be worth a fortune today to the creator of any Broadway show. However, when the artists had worked for Wartheim, they were beginners, but he neglected to tell me that.

"How about if I were looking for something a little less expensive?" I queried.

"Goodbye, nice talking to you, but I'm busy, as you can see," he said suddenly. "Try Howie Hirshhorn. He don't do such great things, but he's a comer."

I don't know how he did it so quickly, but I was on the down elevator as he was still telling me that Hirshhorn was a comer.

Howie Hirshhorn looked more like a goner. Howie seemed to be the kind of a man who had made up his mind years ago that looks mean nothing, that if clothes don't make the man, they shouldn't break him either.

Howie's age was an indeterminate thirtyish and he had

such an ultimate baldness that his bearded chin on that naked head seemed obscene. But he was an engine powered by some internal combustion that probably resulted from too many quick sandwiches and sodas while he worked. His attire consisted of a long sweater and high, wide knit slacks and sandals.

"I can't talk to you right now," he told me, "but if you want to wait while I finish casting this play, O.K." Howie thereby dismissed me to a chair across the office. The office, like Howie, was more concerned with the business than its looks. Actually, it was a poorly lit loft, a rehearsal hall with people scattered throughout, some of them rehearsing skits, sketches and sales pitches.

I was enchanted by the people who came and went, dickering with Howie, discussing various projects with Howie, being seduced by Howie to take a cut in the pay they requested or to work on works they detested.

"Listen, Mary," Howie enjoined a girl who I decided was a human work of art, "do this one. You won't have to do any more parts dealers if you don't want." The girl was twenty-one or twenty-two; she was obviously a dancer and, if not, who cared? She was brilliantly beautiful, with honestly blond hair and a face which must be familiar to you because by now she is a star. If not, fifteen minutes from now.

"Do it, Mary baby, and if that part in the play you want comes up, I'll replace you." Mary was obviously waiting for a part in a real play. Presently, however, she needed Howie's money.

"Howie," her deep Southern tones compelled, "the car parts dealers grab my ass. Those mothers are the biggest schmucks I've ever worked for. Bottlers giggle, medical detail men whistle and stomp, but parts dealers grab ass. You got me working for a third scale. You got me using a phony name so the union can't find me. You got to give me more money. The kind of dough you're paying me I could make working in a hotel room for an hour."

Another illusion shattered, I decided, O.K., so she's not quite a virgin.

"Mary, you never can tell when an agent will see you and say, 'There's Grace Kelly all over again!' " Howie sold.

"Dancing on a forklift in a warehouse? I'm playing before the same kind of guys I left Norfolk for, for chrissakes!"

Then there were Sam and Bill, a writing team who had struggled through a hard season off-Broadway, off off-Broadway and off unemployment compensation. They kept their faces averted whenever I tried to identify them. Their main complaint seemed to be that for $750 Howie wanted a complete show with twelve sketches and seventeen songs about the joys of door-to-door perfume selling by ladies. It was to be an inspirational show to convert new salespeople who had heard the hair-raising stories of the departing salespeople.

"Howie," Sam or Bill, one of them, said, "you know the number to tell 'em not to be afraid to go from house to house? You know 'They Can't Buy It in the Store, but You Can Sell It Door to Door.' Can't we use the music that we used in the insurance show last year?"

"No, boys, some of these women are the same ones who were selling insurance last year." Howie soothed the composers, sold them, and got the promise of the songs and sketches.

"If we weren't on the beach, you could never get us for this kind of money, Howie," Bill or Sam admonished the impresario.

"Boys, I don't mean you no bad intentions, but this is a beachcomber's business. I pick up whoever's on the beach, clean 'em up and make jewelry out of them. Then the big-time boys take over and put my shining little gems in Tiffany's boxes. And at Tiffany prices." The euphemisms seemed to displease Bill and Sam more than pacify them. Howie detected it; he softened. "Boys, better you be my flotsam and jetsam than washed ashore at Warner Newton's."

From Howie's condescending tone I deduced that Warner Newton was many rungs down the ladder of sell-biz attainment from Howie Hirshhorn. Howie corroborated this impression in the curt conversation we had later. When he discovered that I was neither a buyer nor a seller but an asker, he immediately lost interest and rushed back to the assignments his production factory was grinding out.

It was difficult to interview Warner Newton because it was difficult to locate Warner Newton. He apparently found it necessary to move a great deal. His level of production of industrial shows was far less costly and far below that of the others whom we have met. Warner Newton kept his facilities tight and apparently mobile. As his clientele he had small, up-and-coming businesses. Or perhaps businesses which would never come up. But I decided, as Warner Newton must have decided earlier, there is a need for industrial shows at all levels.

Newton's office finally turned up in the West Forties off the Avenue of the Americas. If you are wondering where such a location would be in your town—because there is a Warner Newton in your town—it would be in an old building in the downtown area, squeezed in between a wholesale optical dealer and a small distributor of imported leather goods.

The lettering on the door of Warner Newton's establishment was impressive. It read: "Warner Newton Enterprises, Industrial and Multi-Media Shows. Commercial and Presentation Instruction, Kiddie Parties and Bar Mitzvahs, Private and Stag Bookings, Religious Pageants and Television Acts, School Entertainments and Family Reunions, Animal Acts and Auctioneering." Below the list of impressive callings for which Warner Newton listened was the simple qualification: Warner Newton, Where the Stars Come Out.

His office was also shared by a factory representative of a West Coast ball-bearing concern, a defrocked CPA and a plump lady who did typing for a fee per page and who answered all the phones. Newton's desk was to the rear of the office so that his was a picturesque view of the airshaft.

At the Newton desk sat Newton, a small package wrapped in pin stripes. What a piece of impetuosity Newton was. He fairly leaped across the desk to usher me into his branch of the office. The other occupants ignored the welcoming ceremony as if a wall intervened.

He did not give me time to explain that I was searching the situation, merely investigating the potential of his services.

"Do you know what I did for five thousand dollars for MacCarren's Oil Filters? But how could you know? You would have thought it cost fifty thousand dollars if you saw the show. Three acts showing the filter as the leading item in the oil burner. I created Mac the Oil Filter, a great character played by Ramon Velasquez. Velasquez, the same sonofabitch who is on Channel 47 as Emilio in *La Strada de Dolorosa.* Ha! You see him?" He moved away from his desk and almost danced with glee. Then, no answer expected from me, he continued.

"We sold the shit out of those oil repairmen. They bought those oil filters like they was salamis full of maryjane. I had two semi-nude girls representing Miss Dirty Oil and Miss Clean Oil and I gave every repairman a water gun with detergent to shoot off the oil from Miss Dirty Oil. When she was drenched, she was nude! What a success! Five-piece rock band playing 'Every filter that they take, a repair call you can make!' "

Now he was watching for a reaction. I think the only reaction he detected was fear, so he shifted his approach to a lower key.

"All right, sir! How about thirty-five hundred like the introduction of the new French Fried Alphabets at Chicken Flickin'? I had puppets dressed like alphabet fries, six puppets dancing and singing, 'Raise your profit takeout levels with these greasy little devils!' Ha? The thing was mounted on the back of a truck and we played the music taped by a local rock group—the Zonkers, do you know 'em?—and we toured the tri-state area. The Chicken Flickin' stands sold out those little fried letters like they was oil filters! It was beautiful. Increased morale at the stands by a thousand percent."

I could see that Newton had constructed in his mind a picture of me as a client. But it was impossible to stop him, he seemed to be enjoying his performance so much.

"O.K., what ya got? Two thousand bucks, right? Fifteen hundred? O.K. O.K., for fifteen bills, lemme see." Newton was thinking, mentally drawing in his horns, cutting into his profit margin but still managing to live.

He issued his statement. "For fifteen bills we give you a multi-media bit. A couple slide projectors, a taped-music spectacular while the slides flip in and out, and a live broad with great legs to tap dance in time to the music. What's the product?" But he did not wait for the answer. "Tell you what. We throw in the hall for another three hundred and fifty dollars. There you got it. The food is extra, but the basics is built in. I do the sales stuff for the staff. What is it—salesmen, repairmen, counter-men, lady salespeople? What? What?"

"I'm here for information." I said it as simply as I could. There was no other way and there would probably never be another time. Warner Newton moved back to his desk, sat down heavily on his tired chair. He seemed less animated now that he knew the truth. But he was not dejected.

"All right, I'll show you something." He said it with the air of someone revealing some essential fact to a confidant. "This is what I can do for you. I can get you an accordionist and a sandwich sign for five hundred dollars to tour all of your weak links in the organization. The guy will sing songs of encouragement to the sales force so that by the time he's finished they'll be rarin' to get out and low-ball those suckers in! Five hundred dollars for twenty-four hours of constructive selling impact that will make you proud that you took the magnificent Newton on for the job!"

He settled back, exhausted. It was all over. If I had been afraid of price, he had gone to rock bottom. His organization could stand no more compromise. I told him what I was there for, to provide a background for the field, for people to know the truth, that there were people who when they heard about him would want to avail themselves of his very specialized services. He perked up.

"Kid, lemme tell you something," he exuded. "When they come to me I don't work cheap. Sure, for you I was willing to do a favor. But I got my people, my organization, overhead. Five hundred dollars was a make-believe figure, like when you say 'X Dollars.' I got a good bunch of people. I got to charge."

"I realize that, Newton." What a change had come over him! I felt I had to continue my encouragement. "When they hear about you, they'll all want you and your organization."

"Sure, you know, I got writers, actors, consultants. Costs. And they'll be amazed at the results. With my staff, I can handle the biggest and I may have to turn down the small ones. But there's big money in this biz." He was O.K. again. I felt better.

As I rose to say goodbye he leaned over the desk. "Kid, since you believe in this here so much, I'm gonna let you in on a little secret."

Now he was ready to give me the real information. I sat down again.

"We can make a fortune in this business, but I'm undercapitalized. If you could see your way clear to invest a thousand bucks, you can have half of one of the fastest-growing—"

I really had to go this time. I left with his voice ringing in my ears, "All right, kid, make it five hundred. Five hundred can't break you! Kid, you want to buy some office furnit—"

I closed the lettered door.

CHAPTER TWELVE

. . . Brought to You Live!

Why do you think they began to run around without their pants onstage? Why do you think they shattered the restrictions on what you could show and tell in the theater?

Those of us over thirty yelled, "Why does everything have to be so naked?" as we submitted to the delights of established American voyeurism. We were sneaking peeks at all the interesting things while we were tsk-tsking as our forefathers before us.

And the under-thirties people were defending their new theater, screaming, "Voyeurs! Dirty old men and women! That's not naked, that's nude. Naked is pornographic. Nude is erotic. Naked is a word used for prurient purposes. Nude is when the human form is an erotic symbol or meant to designate the heights of realism."

And we told them, "What's wrong with symbolism and suggestion? What's the big rush for eroticism? Once you see an actor with his everything hanging out, you

know all about him. The mystery is gone; he can no
longer have a mystique. Without his mystique, he has
nothing. Let him try to come onto the stage and impress
us playing *Hamlet* when we have already seen him without his jerkins."

The younger generation drew itself up for the fray.
"What are you making such a big fuss for? It's different
today from when you were a kid. In your day the body
was taboo. But times have changed. Today the body is
part of the scene. The nudity that you used to laugh or
snicker at is accepted by our generation. We're people,
one sex or another, we're people."

"Ho-ho, unisexers," we snickered. (They were right;
we *were* snickerers.) "You think when you see it all you
know it all. A peek is better than a stare, a guess is sexier
than a glare, naked is not so hot as underwear. Sex should
be forbidden a little so that it is sexy. Nothing will be
dirty anymore and that's a shame."

And we told them. We hated to say it, but we told
them. "In our day the theater, the stage was a power-
house, a Titan for ideas and a place to thrash out the
unpopular social notions that might later become popular. We threw economic blasphemies at the system from
the stage. We suggested that God was possibly deceased,
and we let go with a 'goddam' and an occasional 'shit'
that blew everybody's hat off. Why, we even had a show
called *Tobacco Road,* in which an actor turned his back
to the audience and pretended he was pissing in the
windrows."

"We see all that stuff on television on the seven o'clock
news," they told us, growing their hair.

"Well, we didn't have television and we only had an

impotent kind of radio yelling, 'You wanna buy a duck.' And in the movies when two people were going to do it, they fell into the grass clutching and sighing and the camera panned up to the sky."

"But what difference does it make," asks the delightful young actress (twenty-two years old, 38–24–38), "whether you show your body? Art is the thing. It's not whom you are; it's whom you are supposed to be. The body is part of the entire psyche. The soul, the exterior are one. The flesh merely gives form to what's inside you. And we've seen on television what people's insides can do—the hostility, the murder. Nudity is next to cleanliness."

We forgot that we were talking about television for a moment. "Don't you find that standing in front of all those people gives you a funny feeling? Or at least the feeling you're being used?"

She came back with a logical answer. "There may be some conditioning to it. Girls are accustomed to being thought of as an artistic vessel. But a woman wants to show off her body as it expresses nature's artistry."

"Yeah, yeah," we countered.

"What earthly wrong can there be in what the Lord has bestowed if it gives other humans pleasure?"

"I believe, I believe!" I lauded. Then, in a less religious vein: "How did you get into such an uplifting phase of theater?"

"I first heard the call when Edgar, my boy friend, convinced me to share the beauty I had been given with the world. He took some pictures of me and sent them to *Playboy, Penthouse, Scant, Nature Girls* and *Buff.* I made the centerfold and the offers came in for me to share my gift for total fulfillment."

And is your career advancing? we wanted to know.

"Yes indeed." She was very enthusiastic. "I have had four roles since my first New York appearance. In the first show I was in the naked crowd scene. In the second I had a long speech as one of the bathing daughters in *King Lear.* I went on to play Roxanne in *Cyrano as Seen by the Marquis de Sade.* Currently I am in rehearsal as a violated nude nun in a musical version of *The Hunchback of Notre Dame.* So you can see I am making progress."

Is the attitude of men actors who appear nude similar to that of women?

"When people are acting, they are actors. They are being the characters in the drama. The mind must materialize a vision of the character and then make the entire being represent the vision. Nude men on the stage are like women except maybe they flop around a little more." Or so she said.

And the producers who are molding these young people into commercial presentations, are their motives as lofty? Ask the film maker.

"The day has come," he tells us, "to get to the core of things. Our films serve a vast public who needs a more realistic approach to their pictures than before television. We serve the public a release from their pent-up sexual hangups. Masters and Johnson concur with a lot of the Women's Lib broads. Ladies like to be titillated by the same things what hot up men. In regular movies we find ways to insert sex into the story. In exploitation pictures we find ways to insert a story into the sex. We help reduce sex crimes and other physical assaults which come from the sublimination [sic] of sexual drives inherent in all of us. We give them a release from reality."

But, we bored in, you mentioned that your pictures

were more realistic with the sex scene and then you said it was a release from reality.

"Whatya want from me, fella?" he explained. "We got to make a buck. So if it takes a little ass, a little this, a little that, we gotta give them what they can't get on TV."

The *wunderkind* producer of the Broadway and off-Broadway productions which were doing fairly well for live theater, thank you, disagreed vociferously with the film producer. "All we hoped to achieve with nudity and sex participation onstage," he is quoted as saying, "was a greater sense of involvement with the audience, a reaching out to convince them that they can be involved. We had to convey the idea that this was not television; this was a liveness displayed before them."

"Were you successful?" we asked.

"Made a fucking fortune," he explained in depth.

Blame television. Broadway had been the reality show years ago. The stage had been a living forum for the contemporary malaises set to literature, the words and music of happiness and unhappiness. Broadway had burned its bra a long time ago. Now the old girl was forced to drop her slacks to attract a little attention.

Helping to pull down her pants was the movies. The films handled their new position in regard to the inroads of television in a forthright and upstanding manner. First everybody panicked and threatened suicide. Then the forward-thinking movie executives figured out how to compete with television: they sold off all of their backlog of films, hoping to make television so dull that no one would look at it.

When that caper failed, the movies decided to turn honest. It stole Broadway's technique; it became a forum for ideas in depth. The films hysterically fulfilled some of the functions that the theater had performed. But the movies could count on several blessings. There was no proscenium arch to restrict its movement. There were a hundred and one kinky new technological developments to blow the mind of the moviegoer.

Fighting for life, the movies accepted gracefully the new code of morality which said everything went and anything could go. So the movies, swinging from the floor, came up with a combination of ideas and the liberal expression to pursue them. It combined pot shots with crotch shots, and that made tough competition for the living theater.

Broadway was forced to ante up with whatever it could do that the TV and movie cameras couldn't. The stage concentrated on what was inaccessible to the cameras. Live. Wide stage. Happiness. Escape. A little nudity, a little profanity, but mostly happiness.

When the curtain rose, what you saw and heard was a happy extravaganza, pulsating with glittering costumes, inspired settings. But the tunes didn't run through your head; they walked. And the lyrics were pretty pedestrian too. Did I forget the book of the show? So did they. Most writers were heading for Hollywood and steady work in TV. But there were live performers.

If it was not a musical comedy, they put on a comedy comedy.

No angel wanted to lose his assets to provide an artistic triumph that would bother the theater-party ladies and their tired husbands. The poor men had been dragged to the theater with the guarantee that they would not be disturbed with anything significant or noisy. A scrapbook of *My Financial Disaster* makes any theatrical backer wary.

So the angels resorted to tried-and-true formulas. They ordered comedies cut from the same cloth as the television situation comedies. If they felt slightly adventuresome, they imported a tweedy English number that had looked good on London's West End. When a show that had triumphed in a long run in England but was totally inappropriate for New York flopped in one night, they could not understand. "Jeez, it ran so long over there and it's in the same language," they whimpered.

Or they breathed life into an old turkey that had been a huge success in the golden days of Broadway. They hyped the public with a publicity campaign that would have made an award winner out of the good old Black Plague.

They needed the security blanket of knowing that when the curtain went up the second night they were not the only people sitting in the seats.

To tell the truth, it was only 99 percent due to television that the New York live theater went where it went. The economics of the big town were so punishing that the most imaginative things about the shows were their prices.

There were better shows on Broadway outside the theaters. Junkies, hookers and hustlers played their parts with an occasional walk-on by the police. The audience dashed from taxi to theater and from theater to taxi hoping that the worst thing that would happen to them that evening would be the show.

There was a smell of decay about the old Gay White Way.

The young people could not afford the prices, so they managed to do without Broadway. But could Broadway do without them?

Some of the productions summoned the audience onto the stage to participate with the actors. Some of the actors came into the audience to touch the audience. With clothes, without clothes, with half clothes, the far-out dramatic groups attempted to make the audience understand what live theater was all about as opposed to televisionland.

There was a lot of touching, feeling, sensitivity going on. There were small theater groups which used your hangups as the basic material for improvisation of a play—a kind of "Let's make up a couple of scenes about your latent homosexuality" theater. They did plays with dialogue and without dialogue. The experimental theaters opened and shut down with the regularity of a pay toilet.

Much of the procedure of the young theater is a groping, grasping with immense but largely inarticulate devotion. But even with this inability to make sense, some of the young theater is still more exciting and promising than the big-time, dying, living theater, Broadway.

You would expect the youth of television-oriented countries such as ours to be inspired to seek out the remaining places where live entertainment flourishes. And some of them do. Some of them attend the music festivals, fairs, theatricals, tents and small theaters. But much of what they are seeing is live television on tour.

Having been raised on a daily diet of television, perhaps we have a bemuddled outlook on live entertainment. Maybe TV has rattled our brains.

Since reality has been coming to us for so long as a little show on the little screen, we may not recognize what a real-life situation is anymore. We may think that a living, true occurrence is live theater, a live show, and that we are just part of the act.

Otherwise, how to explain the press reports of dozens of horrendous happenings where crowds assemble and do nothing but observe? Occasionally they may applaud or yell "Jump!" but there is evidently no more feeling about these events than if we were watching them on TV. Maybe everybody thinks it's a live show and nobody feels he wants to get involved.

Or maybe it's because everybody knows what happens to people who do get involved. We've seen it on television.

Or is it because we have moved into an era where we have been conditioned by TV to the grimmest dramatic situations as entertainment, just another killing between 7:30 and 10:00 P.M. And if it isn't happening to us, is it really happening at all?

Is this where we are after wending our way out of two decades of war, crime, assassination, revolution, poverty, massacre, space meandering, that we have witnessed as live and taped episodes on TV? In our living rooms as entertainment we have seen everything that people can think of to elevate, subordinate and con each other. Why go out to the theater when you can stay in your warm home and catch the eleven-o'clock riot?

And once you accept the world as your theater it becomes difficult to accept the theater as drama.

Fortunately, theater lovers, there have always been hams. Through rain and snow and gloom of night, there have always been writers and directors and other creative compulsives who want to be involved with hams.

There have always been enough of us to sit down for a moment in the evening to watch the hams, so there will probably always be live theater. But it may not be in New York as Broadway. With the exception of those folks who live in New York it really doesn't matter whether there is a "Broadway" or not. With the rash of performing-arts centers that are pimpling the face of the nation, there will be live theater.

The live theater will have to find some way to coexist with the electronic theater in a system that our very human brains have yet to evolve.

And when those pioneers deliver that new, live entertainment, that innovative drama that can entertain and move people, the theater will have a new form, whatever it is

There will be only one problem. When that new form of live-theater presentation is sculpted and polished and perfected for presentation, will they rush out to sell the rights to television?

CHAPTER THIRTEEN

The Depth of
a Critic

Everything that appears on television is a show. Everything—war, movies, death, children's shows, public-service announcements, puppy dogs, assassinations, cooking, the moon, science, mystery, God, talk, variety, State of the Union messages, commercials, investigations, economic reviews, crime. Anything and anyone that I have omitted, please include.

Here it is, over twenty years since big-time national television crashed through the paper hoop of yesterday, and we still have not solidified our definition of television, what television really is. We know what it has done: It has changed our landscape, it has changed our lives, it has changed our minds. Yet we are still unable to ascertain what it is. It certainly is not what it really is—communications. We corrupted that simplicity from the start.

It is a show. It's either a communications show or a show through communications.

Let me pose the problem of the critics as an example. They are a show. They are probably not even aware of their enigmatic position, so let's make them aware. Why should we be the only ones with enigmatic positions?

First, let us differentiate the critic from the reviewer, if that remains a possibility in this television age. A reviewer, as I define it, reviews a work when it appears and tells us whether to spend the money to see it. A critic has the more arduous task of analyzing the work in regard to its kind. A reviewer tells us whether or not to see it; a critic tells us what it was all about. Before television.

With television came the complications of the show box. Before that time a reviewer—Judith Crist, for example—writing in any of her various outlets, advanced her judgment of whether we should or should not see a film. The drama critic of the New York *Times,* the Washington *Post,* the Chicago *Tribune,* whatever, did the same for the works in his specific domain. Then Judith Crist had the enviable opportunity among her peers of saying her sayings on television. An entirely different set of criteria said hello.

First, whatever physical embellishments Miss Crist feels are required are required: wardrobe, coiffure, make-up. She is *appearing,* physically appearing, and she desires to be seen at her most commendable aspect. How does she enhance what it is she has to say? Why should she have to enhance what she has to say? Because she wants to come off as well as possible, to be as effective as possible, and when she is finished appearing she wants to leave the impression that that Judy Crist is O.K.! Understandable.

Now, at what point is what she says separable from

how she says it? At no point. If she writes it well but says it badly, it is not half so effective as if she were to write it badly and say it well. TV makes of her a performer. She is a show in herself, full of facial expressions, nuances, gestures, a whole performance.

Obviously this is a fictional representation because there could be nobody by the name of Judith Crist. But the same circumstances would control the appearance of any reviewer or critic whether it be Miss Crist, John Simon, Rex Reed or Samuel Boswell. The person appearing on the tube is a performer, and when the performance is unsatisfactory or dull, according to the age-old custom of show business, as expressed in the bejeweled Chronicles of Thespia, that person is not invited for a return appearance.

Some of the critic-reviewers take the stance of being predictably outrageous. That's always good for fun watching. Others take for their routine the demolition of whatever it is they are reviewing. They wield the machete of satirical pruning to the detriment of the unfortunate originator of the piece. The latter reviewer-critic-performer is not interested in the information he is giving the audience so much as he is interested in fulfilling his role as Jo Jo the Art-Wit. At this point he has ceased being the reviewer-critic and has evolved totally into the performer.

The temptation to be a performer engulfs the ego, swirling around with the incense of personal gratification, of being loved by the multitudes, being interesting, being a bitch, being a scamp or teacher, whatever makes 'em love ya. Applause, applause, applause.

The credentials of criticism have been largely invalidated since the beginning of the television era. The critic and the criticized might disagree before, but now they have moved irreconcilably apart. Criticism, at its best, is considered an art form itself, but television never shows it at its best. TV displays not the criticism but the *critic making the criticism.* The critic on television is performing and he is performing his own written works when he is criticizing. He is a whole exhibition, that critic, a whole show in himself. Once he has put on his dancing shoes to go into his act, he is as vulnerable to criticism as the creative work he is about to attack. Picture the novelists, the playwrights, the composers, the lyricists, the actors all sitting and watching and saying, "That dirty . . ."— but each must be saying it in his own happily withering way.

There is a contention loosely running around that says that notwithstanding written or broadcast criticism of a work, word-of-mouth critique is still the final arbiter. These contenders maintain that although the television reviewers, the radio reviewers, the print media folk tear a film, a book, a play to pieces—after all this criticism, the public may still flock to spend their money on the work. Word of mouth will bring 'em in. Such an argument means that criticism is an aid but not a determinant to the success or failure of any creative work. I think that word of mouth, as a contender, has taken the final count.

The old reliable unreliable "they say it's good" or "they say it's lousy" has been transferred from what two or three of your friends say to what two or three electronic critics say. Electronic criticism is immediate. When "they say" it's lousy today, they are the people on TV and radio. The transmission of the word-of-mouth electronic critique has made its impervious impression many hours or days before the edited, delayed responses of the printed reviews come waddling out of their lairs. That impression, that feeling of success or failure is implanted before the papers and the magazines can offer tempting, mitigating appraisals.

And don't be fooled. The demand of the electronic media in the past decade has brought people into critical eminence who are less qualified than you think. Some of them fit their critical analyses in between their other, real, jobs; they just happened to walk out of the elevator at the right time. Many of them turn back to bumpkins at midnight when they go back to their regular assignments.

Some of the best reviewers and critics are some of the worst performers. When they appear on television on a regular basis they destroy their validity and themselves. And some of the best performers are some of the worst critics.

If you want to fight about it, you might question the ineptitude of some of the critics by asking, "If they're so bad, how did they get on there in the first place?"

My considered answer: "God knows." The very fact that they are there dignifies the critics with the seal of authenticity. Just being on TV or radio makes them a TV or radio critic. There is an old radio-TV saying that I reveal here for the first time: "If you're still on the air the second day, you are what you claim to be."

Consider the situation of the expensive production arriving in town, all participants having done what they think they should have done, having spent what they had to spend, awaiting the onrushing hordes of viewers bringing cash. The comedian TV reviewer sees the production, sees a chance for a couple of great gags, goes in front of the TV cameras to face his adoring devotees and gives a *tour de force* performance at the expense of the production.

Instantly, the prospective audience of the production has a picture of the critic and his production but not necessarily a valid picture of the *production*. If they are a knowledgeable, perceptive audience, they will await the press reviews or the corroboration of other critics. But no matter what kind of audience they are, some damage has been done. The reviewer on the ten-o'clock or eleven-o'clock news, blindfolded, can shoot an arrow right into the heart of the producer of a movie or play. And on a network presentation, a reviewer can kill from New York to Los Angeles and all points intervening simultaneously.

There are ancillary dilemmas of criticism imposed by the appearances of performing critics on television. Suppose you have an example of one of the newer, with-it graduates of the mod school of criticism. When Mr. Hip appears on television with his dashing message of see and slash, his vast mustache and longer-than-average tresses flowing in the electrons, his image is immediate. The reaction to his image is almost as immediate. His aficionados will welcome him; the middle-of-the-roaders will wonder and the conservative reviewers will be repelled. Before that reviewer or critic has had a chance to say his piece, he has prejudiced his audience one way or the other. And we have established an understanding gap.

With the proliferation of onstage appearances made possible for analysts by this great electronic TV of a mouth, does it mean that we are going to need minority

reviewers? Faced with the bubbling struggling of minor-
ities, can any reviewer-critic be a woman or a man for all
segments? Is it possible that there has erupted the need
for specialists to appraise the works of creative people
from diverse points of view? Should there not be a female
eviewer, a black reviewer, a homosexual, an Indian,
Spanish, youth reviewer, as well as a typical 100 percent
non-affiliated reviewer? Or are such considerations the
subject for another time, another book, another nut?

Haven't we got enough of a problem just trying to be
real people, confronted as we are by this machine that
makes everybody a performer? Even performers.

Let's drop a few names. Bob Hope, Paul Newman,
Bill Cosby, John Wayne, Jane Fonda. There they were,
stepping out of the characters they had assumed in films,
onstage and in TV drama to come forward and speak as
their political and civic selves. They marched across the
TV screen to the left, the right and down the middle,
trying to establish themselves as real folks, to demonstrate that they were citizens with a point of view. And
what happened?

We continued to see them as Bob Hope, Paul Newman, Bill Cosby, John Wayne and Jane Fonda. As
players. Just as we saw the President and the Mayor as
performers. Just as we saw everything else that came on
at the switch of a knob as a show. And we sat there, unintentionally judging their performances on our mental
ratings systems. Another show.

No wonder our young people have been so confused
—and confusing to us. They have lived in televisionland
all their lives. They have been educated by television
shows before they stepped inside the little overcrowded

strife-torn classroom. Twenty years ago when you entered school you knew where the candy store was, where to meet your mother after school and that you had to hold it in until class was over.

Now our canny little five-year-olds know how to read, where Indochina is, where the Middle East is split and the symptoms for congenital syphilis and ODing. They have seen it all on the screen machine.

What they don't understand is reality. What is a real person and what is a performer. And with their callow way of youth they *tell* us they don't know.

We don't know what's real either, but we are certainly not going to tell them that we don't know.

How can anybody know when there are so many microphones and cameras waiting to record and play back everything we say and do? You never know when you're going to be on, so you might as well be "on" all the time.

All because we wanted a little home picture-show machine. What we didn't realize was that we were going to be in the picture.

So how can you tell a real person from a performer when television has made us all performers?

If you figure it out, if you can figure out how to be a real person, you will be a very salable commodity.

And if you do, can I be your agent?